The proceeds from the sale of this book go to support the Ski Museum of Maine and the Maine Ski Hall of Fame

# We Jumped

By

Robert Lee Remington

&

Thomas K. Remington

~~~~~

Edited by Steve Trinward

ISBN-13:978-1514734247

ISBN-10:1514734249

# Acknowledgments

Long conversations to swipe away the cobwebs of memory could not produce all that is contained within the pages of this book. Friends and publications provided dates, places, names and other information. We wish to thank Mike Stowell, a former Maine ski jumper, for his prompt historic information on the Elm Street Jump in Andover, Maine; Bruce Simmons, ski jumper, for taking the time to find answers involving ski jumping history in Andover; Don Angevine, ski jumper, for some forgotten events in the Bethel region; Richard Paradis for old newspaper clippings and information concerning his father's ski repair business in South Paris; Richard Kent and his book *Words for a Mountain*; Don Bennett's *Bethel Journals*; Robert Spidell's *Andover Maine* history; and numerous Internet website pages and archived newspaper publications.

# Foreword

My family lived in the Virginia section of Rumford, a hillside community above the waterfalls of the Androscoggin River, about 25 miles east of the Remingtons' home in Bethel. Each winter, just like the Remington clan, we built a ski jump in our backyard. On any given winter's day in the early 1960s, a gaggle of neighborhood kids lined the slope competing for the farthest jump. It's what we did, day in and day out, when snow blanketed the mountains of western Maine.

When we weren't competing, we spent hours sprucing up that jump. With a massive metal shovel, one of the older boys would square off the front and sides of the jump. Then, wearing woolen mittens, another kid would smooth out the rough edges making it *just so.* Strapped into skis, the rest of the crew packed from outrun to takeoff in tight little sidesteps that left the snow looking like wide-wale corduroy. We took pride in that rippled effect, and always retraced our steps if we slipped and broke the pattern.

We planted 3- to 4-inch spruce twigs all the way up both sides of the jump creating a pathway to guide our descent. Then, spruce needles were tossed to the center of the landing hill to aid the jumper's perception. On a hill as small as ours these needles were merely window dressing, but spruce needles on the landing hill looked official and that's what mattered. Finally, centered on the lip of the jump, wide enough for a set of skis to pass through, two more evergreen sprigs cued the jumper's liftoff.

The most skillful skier among us set first tracks. That jumper, confident and steady, kept a flat ski, never wobbled, and left a picture-perfect pathway across the corduroy and down through the spruce sprays at the end of the jump. Back then, we all admired the track setter. Still do.

I remember my first official jumping meet. Cub Scout Pack 181 held the event in March 1962 next to Sunnyside Terrace Cemetery on what we called, with a wild-west swagger, the Tomb Road. I'm betting that Red Bulger and Porky Cyr cleared the brush and built the jump between working shifts at the paper mill. As 7- to 10-year-olds, we lined up for practice jumps desperate to win one of the ribbons that our den mothers displayed near the carafe of piping hot chocolate and the mountain of sugar donuts fresh from Freddie's Restaurant. On one side of the landing hill, making the meet altogether official, several fathers with long sticks marked our jumps and called out the distances. "Eighteen feet!" "Twenty-one feet!"

I still have my white, third-place ribbon from the meet and the memory of those donuts, that jump, and my friends.

Bob and Tom Remington's *We Jumped* conjures up those long-ago days of ski jumping. Their stories transported me back in time to a family like my own who *lived* skiing. While reading the brotherly banter, I felt compelled to write my oldest brother, the real ski jumper in our family. A veteran flyer of Rumford's monstrous jump known as *The Suicide*, Allen initiated my brother Robert and me on the 20-meter hill at Black Mountain. We were 10 and 12 years old, and these days when I hike the area where that jump once stood, I picture the O's our mouths formed as we glided out over the knoll.

As you read this collection of stories, you'll picture Bob and Tom's dad, *Rockin' Chair* Remington, chatting it up with his ski-flying friends next to a large wooden jump. When you read the lively back-and-forth between these two brothers, you'll get the feeling that you're sitting in a ski lodge or wedged in at the Remington's supper table sharing stories of the longest jumps, the wax that worked, and their plans for the next day's jump on the hills of western Maine. Through their words, you will also come to know their remarkable family.

There are no pretensions in this book, just the plain-spoken voices of two good guys—brothers—former ski jumpers, sons of a ski jumper, trading memories for a good cause.

Richard Kent

Rumford, Maine

# Introduction

I believe that history becomes more important to us as we age. My mother recently gave me her writings from many years ago. It told of her childhood, and the times in which she lived were fascinating. My father passed in 1975 at the young age of 51. At 26 years in age, I didn't realize how much it would have meant many years later to know more about him and his childhood and experiences before my time.

Several years after his passing, Mom told me about his days in skiing. She told of an exceptional four-event skier with an amazing gift in the cross country event. He won races by minutes. He was unbeatable as a racer at Andover High School. He was offered a scholarship by UNH and was to be the roommate of Ralph Townsend and Ed Styrna. Townsend went on to become a member of the 1948 US Olympic Nordic Combined team, legendary coach at Williams College, and was inducted into the US Ski Hall of Fame in 1975. Ed Styrna, the legendary track coach at UMaine, an outstanding track athlete, received his induction into the Maine Running Hall of Fame in 1999.

When our team traveled to Williams College for their winter carnival in 1972, Ralph Townsend sought me out when he saw my name on the start list. He asked me if I was one of Clarence Remington's sons. I was not surprised. It happened frequently. "How is Rockin' Chair?" he asked. I said, "Good," as always. I didn't know Dad would live only three more years.

Forty years later, I regret that I didn't have the foresight to realize that one day I would want to know every little detail associated with his times. How did he get his start in skiing? What did he use for equipment? Who coached him? How did he train? And, of course, each of these questions would lead to many more.

Why didn't he accept that UNH scholarship? He fell in love, got married, and raised a family. He never looked back. Did he ever regret his decision? If he did, he never show it.

What you are about to read comes from what my brother and I could remember of our days in ski jumping. After months of pondering, we decided that we wanted to provide a "feeling" for what it was like growing up on skis in Western Maine in the 1950's, '60's, and '70's. In so doing, we chose ski jumping for it was a passion-filled sport which is sadly missing from the lives of our youth in the 21st century. In this day of enthusiasm for extreme winter sports, why isn't ski jumping part of that culture in the winter wonderland of the state of Maine?

Though I am a retired teacher and ski coach at age 66, I have not yet considered working on my 'bucket list' but when I do, I know of two items that will be on that list.

1: I hope this book sells millions of copies. All profits of the selling of this book will go to the Ski Museum of Maine. We need to preserve our history.

2: Before I pass I would like to stand beside the outrun of a ski jump in the great state of Maine with  many of my ski jumping peers and witness a ski jumping competition.

We thank you for your donation to the Ski Museum of Maine and hope you thoroughly enjoy your journey into the past.

Robert Lee Remington

# In the Beginning

**Tom:**

It must have been a right of passage; a transition from crawling to skiing. Maybe that is a slight exaggeration, but certainly nothing that I was aware of at the time. As a matter of fact it wasn't until later in life that I realized that attaching some apparatus to my feet and playing in the snow, morning, noon, and night wasn't a typical human behavior, especially compared to today's standards of normalcy.

I'm reflecting back on nearly 60 years, at a time of living a mostly isolated life, deep in rural Western Maine. As such, how was I to know what others did in their spare time? I suppose that what I didn't know didn't hurt me. As I age, I see that what I didn't know helped me.

Didn't everybody ski?

Reliving in many ways everything ski jumping, I've come to realize what an impact it had on my life. During conversations with my brother I became increasingly excited about resurrecting some of the skiing events and locations of those memories, with the intent of capturing moments in skiing history. Not necessarily to capture a complete history, but simply from our perspectives.

The following are my brother Bob's (Rem) and my perspectives on growing up on skis in Maine. What I write comes from my memory. Bob lies so I don't know where his will come from.

I'm sure I won't get it all right, but many of the minor details, omissions, and mishaps shouldn't take away from the basic truth. I hope that statement will clear me of any future guilt or accusations.

I will provide as much detail as I can on events that I was personally involved in and share what I remember of those that I may have not been a direct part of. I will recall the names, many of whom were the greats in their ski sports of the day, and I'm sure I'll leave some out. I mean to not offend anyone. Please enjoy what we can recall.

# The Venue

**Tom:**

Bethel, Maine, where we grew up, was about as close to the center of all things as one could get. Maine humorist, Joe Perham, always declared that West Paris - which is not that far from Bethel - was the center of the Universe: it was just exactly half-way between Quebec City, Canada and Boston, Massachusetts.

Western Maine had mountains and hills and a few of the smaller ones surrounded our humble home on the East Bethel Road. That tiny, four-roomed house, nestled into the center of our own skiing venue, our center of the universe, the most of which was littered with hand-built ski jumps, ski trails, ramps, tunnels and a state of the art bobsled run – well, maybe disregard the bobsled run but we did slide a lot. If there was a slope, we built a jump on it. We sometimes wondered if we could negotiate a jump with enough speed to clear the East Bethel Road. To my knowledge that never happened – although I don't remember ever being told what happened to two brothers whose names I didn't even know. Oh, well.

Dad was a ski jumper. It's what he loved to do. Therefore, subjected to the lifestyle I've partially described above, logic would rule that the four Remington boys would ski and be ski jumpers. Dad – Clarence, Clancy, Remmy, Rockin' Chair, Hambone – lived for winter weekends and a ski jumping event somewhere. It could have been Andover, Rumford or Bethel in Maine, Laconia, Littleton, Lebanon, Franconia or Berlin in New Hampshire, Salisbury in Connecticut, perhaps Brattleboro in Vermont, or a trip to Three Rivers, Quebec, Canada.

As little "Rockin' Chairs" we were in training. Snow belonged to the Remington brothers or maybe we belonged to the snow. We always heard that winters were long and dark. There was never enough time during winter. Night after night, we played outside in the snow. Mom would stick her head out the door and begin the call, "Yoooohooooo! Time to come in! Yoooohooooo! Time for bed!" At that familiar sound we would quietly escape to a snow fort, behind a snow bank, into an igloo or farther up a tree. Never did we answer the call.

An incline required a ski jump. There was one just off the side of the lawn; small but it worked...at least for a time. Across the road and east, toward the well house was a good hill. Ergo, a jump, but the landing hill was on the flat but it didn't deter us.

"The Jump" stood directly across the road from the house and on the side of the biggest hill. Dad had confiscated, from who knows where, some old lumber. With a combination (or salad?) of that lumber, saplings, brush and virtually anything we could find, we constructed a jumping hill. The landing had so much brush piled up that when we landed on it, it more closely resembled a trampoline. Oh, well, more fun. Right?

The challenge of finding a good place to start from required determination. We had to maneuver around while hanging onto an available tree, get our skis headed basically in the right direction, and let go. The braver we were, the higher we went for a start. The higher we went the more trees to duck under and go around on our way to the end of the take-off.

Speed. When to know what was enough and too much. Flying higher and farther was what it was about. Perhaps we flew 10 feet, 15, 20? In my mind it could have been the Holmenkollen - and sometimes we pretended it was.

**Robert:**

For the first 13 years of my life I was known as Robert. It wasn't until I was in high school that I suddenly became Bob so, for now, I'm Robert. In response to my esteemed brother's comment that I lie, I will just say that my memory isn't very good (probably too many concussions) but, if I get any information wrong it's simply because I 'miss-remember'. Case in point: I had completely forgotten the jump that was near the well house.

We favored the well-house jump when feeling adventurous. It ran parallel to the road and started at the top of a rise beside and maybe 10 to 15 feet above the road. From that point we could see approaching traffic – please understand that in the 1950's the rare event of an approaching automobile along such a rural route created excitement for all.

If we gauged the speed of the approaching auto just right, we could be airborne at the very moment the unsuspecting motorist passed and the thrill increased when moving along side the automobile while looking down on its roof. I don't remember causing any problems for the motorists but I'm sure Tom will remember if we did since he and Alan were the troublemakers of the family.

For those readers who are not familiar with the method used to determine the size of a ski jump, let's make it as simple as we can and just say, "The size of a ski jump is determined by how far one can safely jump." The key word is 'safely'. It is understood that it is safe to jump to a point on the landing hill somewhere before the slope starts to transition toward the flat. So, a 30-meter jump would be large enough to allow a jumper to fly through the air and land safely 30 meters from the end of the take off. I realize that this is over simplification but it serves the purpose.

The well-house jump would have to be classified a 2-meter since 3 meters would put us on flat ground. Probably a minimum jump for us was 5 meters. That's right; we always landed on flat ground(and usually crashed). We also had to deal with an obstacle. The reason we called it the well-house jump is that a footpath from the road to the well house crossed the path of the jump. If you are wondering why a footpath, it's because we did not have running water and we carried water in 5-gallon pails from the well to the house. When I say *we* carried the water, I think I mean *me*. I don't really remember anyone else carrying water.

The only jump that might have actually been on our property was the one that started on the edge of our side lawn and went down a gradual hill toward the Androscoggin River. An open space occupied an area about 10 feet wide and 100 feet long surrounded mostly by poplar trees with a few alders and pine mixed in. The simple task of piling up snow and shaping it into a takeoff made this an easy jump to maintain. We probably could have safely jumped 15 meters but there was no way to get enough speed so we were limited to jumps more in the range of 2 to 6 meters( 6 for me; 2 for my brothers). This was clearly the safest of the three jumps and, therefore, the most boring. Some of my fondest memories are of nights that we jumped under the light of a full moon.

A nicely designed jump would include an out-run that would gradually transition from flat to slightly uphill allowing for an easy chance to stop. "The Jump" had an out-run that gently sloped down hill all the way to the bank which was at the edge of the road. Failure to stop meant one would sail over the bank and end up in the middle of the road. Intentionally falling down solved that problem.

My most vivid memory of this jump resulted in two sprained knees. Getting good ski equipment was difficult for us and we had to make do with what Dad could come up with. (More about equipment later.). One day, my bindings refused to cooperate. After messing with them for longer than I wanted, I convinced myself that they were in working order. I climbed to the individual-skier-determined starting point and put on my skis. After using a large tree to hold myself, while I got my skis headed in a downhill direction, I pushed off the tree and crouched into my in-run position. I timed the take-off perfectly and carried enough speed that I instantly knew that I was going to out jump the man-made hill and land on nearly flat ground. As I soared out over the knoll and started to lean forward, I realized that I had no skis! I made a quick decision, deciding to try to make it safely without the skis. My quick plan to land in an upright position and try to run down the gradual slope failed. I sank knee deep in the snow as my skis passed me by. Since I, technically, did not fall down, I considered it a new hill record – probably 60 feet.

**Tom:**

Hill record? Phfft! I did warn you. He was a legend in his own mind. But I did dislike The Jump mostly because you couldn't stop, especially when the snow got hard and icy. In those days we didn't have skis with steel edges and the bottom edges of the skis we had, aside from often being mismatched, had worn out edges (rounded over wood).

Perhaps there is another reason for me disliking this jump. One cold day out on the same hill with saucers and double-runner sleds, Robert talked me into putting my tongue on the metal bar at the front of the sled.

At the East Bethel skiing venue, a.k.a. The Center of the Universe, we did other things on winter snow besides ski jump. Yes, there was sledding and downhill skiing as well. More dangerous than the downhill run at Kitzbuhel, the E. Bethel run pushed the envelope beyond the capabilities of antique equipment. I mean our equipment made antique look new.

By today's standards, no mom could find enough "safety equipment" to protect the entrant to the East Bethel Downhill. Any parent allowing such irresponsible activities would be sentenced to life in prison. Back then, for Mom, it was just another day; another "why don't you boys go out and play" day.

With the exception of the hairpin turn at the most critical point of the race, dangers associated with the downhill run were minimal.

An old trail, situated to the side of The Jump, ran up along the side of the hill to an old farm at the top. Maybe 6 to 8-feet wide, although it seemed bigger. Packing the snow on the downhill run required work and ambition – the higher the start, the more work. It didn't get done that often. Climbing up and skiing down served us well.

The run down this trail was the best. Once we entered the small clearing – the same gradual downhill outrun of The Jump – we had to be on our toes to set up for the turn to the right. The 120 degrees that we had to negotiate, combined with ducking beneath the guy cable that held back the electric pole sitting on top of the bank - there was no going around it – caused whoops of excitement to echo through the cold air from a successful run.

If we didn't hang ourselves, we prayed that we could negotiate the turn well enough that we didn't sail down over the embankment and land in the road. "Carving" of turns was out of the question and most of the time we came out of our bindings before getting to the corner.

If we successfully negotiated the corner, the rest was quite boring unless we carried our speed down, and over the well-house jump.

It occurs to me now, as I write, that the Remingtons hosted a winter carnival at the East Bethel venue. We made first, second and third place ribbons for each of the events, i.e. jumping, downhill and something that might have more resembled what today is called glade skiing; only more trees than glade.

Growing up a ski jumper wasn't always about being outside building and playing on jumps. We carried it into the house, but not in the way you might think. One of our favorite pastimes was playing at being at a big hill ski jumping event with all the big names in the sport. Video games, cell phones and the like hadn't even been invented. As a matter of fact, we never really had a television for many years and when we did, we only got one channel. So we created our own entertainment.

Perhaps to Mother's chagrin, we stole her wooden clothespins and took them apart. (Dare I have needs to explain to readers what a clothespin is?) One side of a clothespin, in our minds, replicated a pair of jumping skis. We tried putting two pieces side by side but it was more difficult to go through all the contortions we thought necessary to simulate an actual ski jumper in motion.

Holding the clothespin piece between the thumb and pointer finger - the jumping hill most often being the back of the couch - we could manipulate the fingers and wooden clothespin to simulate the motion of "pressing" out over our fantasy skis. (Note: This is probably when Robert believed he was setting a new hill record for longest jump.) If nobody occupied one of the favored chairs, we might take the cushions and arrange them the best we could to create a jumping hill.

As we each took our turn at jump acting, we would also do our own play by play and even some color commentating. God we were good.

When it was time to play clothespin ski jumping, we scrambled to get first dibs on which ski jumper we wanted to be. I liked to be Ansten Samuelstuen. Maybe the reason I chose this name was because I actually learned to pronounce the name. Calls would go out to be Art Tokle or Art Devlin or, a few times, Ray Roy or Aurelle Legere from Rumford. There were many others.

To complete the show, we should have had red, white and blue banners and John Phillip Sousa march music playing . I wonder what Dad thought of our shenanigans.

**Robert:**

A quick note: Tom always got last dibs. After all, he *was* the youngest.

The downhill run that Tom describes was the precursor to the modern day sport of ski cross. Every time it's televised, I tell my wife that ski cross would have been my event.  Going as fast as you can over jumps and around turns that allow the skier to take a myriad of paths to get to the finish line before the others would have been just perfect for me.

We made use of another ski hill during winters that offered plenty of snow. You know, the kind of winters when the snow banks were way over our heads and we had to walk to school during sub-zero blizzards, uphill – in both directions? The driveway at our home was not very long, although as a kid it seemed to stretch on for miles because we had to shovel all of it. And, again, when I say *we*, I actually mean *me* because I don't remember anyone else shoveling.

The town plow left banks of snow at the entrance to the drive and we shoveled the snow onto one of two mounds located on either side of the drive. I do not exaggerate when I say that those mounds were often piled in excess of ten feet.

The mound of snow located on the east side of the drive was a magnificent location for playing one of our favorite games, King on the Mountain. Sonny, Alan, Tom(my 3 brothers) and I gathered at the top of the 'mountain'. On an agreed upon signal, we tried removing each other from the mound. (The 'agreed upon signal' was usually a 3-2-1-go count down, but someone would always 'go' at 2.) The person remaining alone at the top earned the title of king. Sonny, the oldest – 3 and a half years older than me – usually won(because we let him) and the action often segued into wrestling matches.

So, you ask, "What does this have to do with skiing?" It's simple. Playing King on the Mountain packed the snow down which made it that much easier to pile more snow on top after the next snow storm. In time, it was high enough and firm enough to ski on. We could start at the top, ski down and across the lawn to the jump that was situated just off the edge of the lawn. We didn't really gain any more speed for the jump but it did provide us a longer run.

The snow mound on the west side of the drive became the designated area for snow forts and tunnels. We spent many hours burrowing around underneath that mound of snow. It's a small miracle that one of us didn't end up buried there. We didn't give it a second thought at the time. What did this mound have to do with skiing? Nothing.

A vision came to mind when Tom wrote of the winter carnival we put on for the neighborhood. In it, I'm holding many blue ribbons.

# Equipment and Clothing

**Tom:**

Let's clear up a few issues before moving on. I did *all* the snow shoveling. I carried *all* the water in buckets, all too often feeling much like Gunga Din but not liking it very much. And just to remain accurate in these historic accounts, I won *all* the blue ribbons. As a matter of fact, I won blue, red and white in the same event. So, there!

Both Robert and I have dropped a few subtle hints to this point in order to let readers know that we grew up very poor. "How poor where we?" Poverty around our house was so common that we didn't know it had a name. And because we were poor, ski equipment was difficult to come by. I believe my very first pair of skis was also my three older brothers' first pair. They must have been generic; I don't recall any logo or brand name on them. They had pointed tips – a trademark of embarrassment as newer skis evolved and got rid of the pointed tip.

The foot harnesses comprised a couple strips of brittle leather (it may have been rubber, perhaps from a tire's inner tube or a canning jar), tacked onto the top of the ski. Judging from the construction of the ski, the original harness remained attached to the ski through a slot, about mid-ski, that was about 2 or 3 inches long that went all the way through the ski from the sidewalls. With what we had to work with, nailing the straps to the top of the ski sufficed.

There were also laces, perhaps rawhide, more than likely hay baling twine, that could be loosened or tightened to "adjust" to compensate for the foot or boot.

I have previously mentioned that our equipment was already antique in the 1950s. Some of it may have been left behind by the Vikings. What we had for skis, sleds, boots, clothing, etc. came to us by way of getting it for nothing or by swapping something. Dad always managed to find something for us to play with. As you will discover later in this book, Clarence spent a lot of time and effort gathering ski equipment, not just for himself and his children, but for any kid in the area who had need.

If we could have figured a way to put a bend in one end of a board, we would have sanded it up and made a ski out of it. The original pair of skis, with the pointed tips, was nothing more than two strips of bare wood. Perhaps, once upon a time, there was some kind of smooth surface or preservative on them but there surely wasn't when we played with them.

The act of attaching skis to the feet and sliding downhill constitutes the basic principle of skiing. Certainly this feat is better accomplished if the skis actually slide. Sliding anything on bare ice is a relatively easy task, but trying to slide a dry piece of wood on soft, fluffy snow isn't exactly fun. If that snow happens to be wet and sticky, 6 or 8 inches will build up on the bottom, leaving a frustrated little boy unwilling to play.

The bottoms of our first pair of skis contained a center groove; somebody thought a ski needed a groove down the middle, end to end, to help the ski track in a straight line. Of course today, most skis don't have a groove because, other than a downhill racer, few skiers have a need to go in a straight line.

I'm guessing the skis were made from ash or, perhaps hickory. Age and hours of use wore the softer parts of the wood between the heavy grains into ample grooves. If the direction of the grain was tip to tail, the ski tracked in a straight line. If not, watch out!

There were no edges of steel or hard plastic along the ski bottom that helped to make a turn, particularly on hard snow.

That's the way it was and we liked it. As time passed, we were able to gather equipment. Each time a new item came into the home, it was a bit newer and better. When any of the four of us showed signs of wanting to get a bit serious about ski jumping, Dad upped his efforts to find something we could use for jumping skis.

Jumping skis had three, four or five grooves running the length of them, after all, jumpers did want to track in a straight line riding down the in-run and the grooves provided some stability when landing on the snow-covered hill, keeping the skis from sliding side to side.

Steel edges were not needed for jumping skis. The only turning was for stopping at the end of the outrun. Some ski jumps, like ours at "The Venue," did not provide ample distance to fully slow down and stop, resulting in many mishaps.

A ski jumper needed fast skis. The more speed a jumper could find the farther down the hill he could sail. As we grew, we learned how to take care of, repair, redo and work on our skis, using the latest in technologically developed compounds to apply to the bottoms of jumping skis, to make them go faster.

**Robert:**

Tom's depiction of our ski equipment is accurate. Sometimes the low quality of what we used was the cause of much frustration. I recall many times suffering with trying to get the boots and bindings to work together. We used a number of different designs of toe-plates that operated by having some sort of metal 'catch' hook on to the sole of the boot and hold the boot in the binding. This method worked well except when the boot had worn to the point that the edges of the soles were nearly non-existent or had started to peel away in layers. But through all the years of using hand-me-downs and discarded equipment, we learned appreciation. I don't recall that we ever complained about what we had nor did we ever beg for something better. We stood in our skis at the top of ski jumps next to fellow competitors using much better equipment and we simply took it as what it was: we were using the best gear that our parents could provide for us; we had fun; we were happy!

Fun was clearly the name of the game and sometimes we needed change. Previously, I wrote about introducing ski cross long before it ever became a recognized sport. Such is the case with freestyle skiing and it involved barrel staves. For you younger readers, the wooden pieces that are used to make a barrel are called staves. We had a small barrel at our home for years. It was used to store old nails.

We took the barrel apart. Each stave was a bit more than two feet long, probably five inches wide at the middle, and narrowed to three inches in width at each end. Of course, there were no flat surfaces as the staves curled from tip to tail and from side to side. As a matter of fact, there was no way to tell the tip from the tail until we put the bindings on them. That's right. We mounted ski bindings on them.

What a blast! We skied down the hill forward, backward, sideways. We could spin in any direction. We could jump, do splits, anything the mind could imagine. But the fun was limited by the fact that our feet would begin to ache because the shape of the staves would press our arches in a reverse direction.

**Tom:**

I grew fond of the barrel staves. I can't say it did much to prepare me to be a ski jumper, except maybe strength and balance, but it was fun. It wasn't easy staying upright on those things. We need to credit our brother, Alan, for most of the engineering feats, crafting barrel staves into usable ski toys. He was and always has been the most mechanically inclined in the family. (Note – Robert did not "invent" barrel staves. Sometimes we let him think a lot of things about himself. It's easier and safer that way.)

I recall one day when Alan took the barrel staves to Mt. Abram Ski Slopes. All eyes were focused on him and his "odd" ski things.

With additions to our inventory of confiscated bindings and binding parts, we were able to equip the staves with "bear trap" bindings. The old bear trap binding, I assume called that in reference to once you've gotten yourself cabled and strapped in, much like a bear in a jawed bear trap, there was no escaping. However, who cared about safety releases. As a matter of fact, I do believe we seriously thought about screwing or bolting boots or shoes onto skis and staves to rescue us from the constant battles we fought with skis while wallowing waist deep in powder snow.

After we sanded the bottoms of the barrel staves, we coated them with several layers of shellac, lightly sanding in between coats. Once the bottoms were glossy, hard and slick, it made maneuvering in the snow that much more challenging, as well as fun.

Our jumping skis required proper care and my brothers and I learned how by watching Dad take care of his. The older skis had a painted top surface. Northland made skis and anyone was fortunate to be able to own a pair.

Looks were one thing. Speed was another. The bottoms needed the most attention. They had to be kept in tip-top shape for maximum speed. It helped to have knowledge of how to wax for changing conditions. For many years, shellac was the preferred base coat. As with the barrel staves, several coats with light sanding did the trick.

I'm not sure exactly where the shellac came from but you took your life into your own hands if you spilled it or wasted it. It was treated like gold. No runs, no drips, no errors as the saying goes.

Over time, the shellac built up on the ski bottoms. With age, use and temperature fluctuations, it began to crack. That meant reduced speed, so the shellac had to come off. Dad showed us how to remove it. A piece of window glass with a perfectly cut, straight edge worked precisely to scrape off the old shellac – tip to tail. Of course, it didn't get the shellac out of the groves so sandpaper, steel wool and elbow grease took care of that. Once the surface was clean and smooth, the process of applying the shellac to the bottoms was repeated.

I don't know how my mother put up with all of this. When it was time to work on skis, the kitchen chairs served as a work bench. Skis would be turned upside down, tips hanging just over the top of the back of the chair and scraping was from tip to tail, down to the floor. When that was completed, it was easier to sand by placing both skis between two chair backs. Applying the shellac was better, as well, on a relatively flat surface. I'm sure we must have splattered the floor with shellac. Life was simple.

Timing was critical to make sure we had our skis completed and ready for the next competition. Many nights during the winter months, our house was saturated with the pungent aroma of shellac. I can smell it now.

But shellac eventually gave way to technology. The next generation of jumping ski bases was a product call Ebonite. As the name suggests, the material was black. Ski preparation replicated much the same as for shellac except for a very careful painting of the Ebonite onto a clean, wood base. Of course, the smoother and more uniform the coating, the more speed could be obtained. I recall that Ebonite had a different, acrid kind of odor to it that really wasn't all that pleasant.

Ebonite was faster on snow than shellac and seemed to remain a faster base under more snow conditions. It was hard and durable and didn't crack the way shellac did.

Over time, the evolution of the technology of ski base composites changed. I remember the first time I saw a pair of jumping skis with bright yellow "Kofex" bottoms. The material was one of the first plastics that was used. Everything changed and bottoms got better and better and faster and faster. Even under rapid and extreme changes in weather, the new composites, along with newer and better waxes, improved the quality of the sport tremendously.

As with any ski, jumping skis were not infallible. Ski jumping sometimes involved nasty falls in combination with broken skis. Dad was a regular customer at Paradis' ski repair in South Paris. Henry Paradis was a genius at repairing broken skis and sometimes Dad found some great deals on skis he could bring home and/or share throughout the neighborhood.

After communicating with Henry Paradis' son, Richard, about his father's ski repair and manufacturing business, he sent me a newspaper clipping dated March 14, 1962. The column states that Paradis had 40 years of ski manufacturing experience and planned to operate his business year round. Evidently he was the only business in New England that repaired wooden skis. I'm sure many skiers and ski jumpers of that by-gone era, recognize the Paradis name and the work of Henry Paradis.

## Beyond "The Venue"

**Robert:**

In time, we began using our home venue less and less as competitions at other sites piqued our interest - places as far away as Andover and Rumford. The number of cross-country (x-c) ski races we entered prior to our high school years were few and limited mostly to races held as part of winter carnivals. The Pineland Ski Club in Andover sponsored skiing competitions as part of Andover's Winter Carnival and the Chisholm Ski Club did the same for their Winter Carnival in Rumford.

The first jumping competition we entered was on a jump located behind the town hall in Andover. The land behind the town hall extended nearly 75 yards before it dropped sharply to the flood plain of the Ellis River. That drop provided a well-shaped landing hill for a 20-meter jump. A wooden structure that neared 25 feet in height served as the in-run and takeoff. The builders did a great job shaping and positioning the tower providing an excellent chance to get in good jumps that would follow the contour of the landing hill.

A set of wooden steps ran up the left side parallel to the in-run tracks. We removed our skis, placed the bottoms together, and flung them on to one shoulder. Using one hand, strategically located along the length of the skis to balance them on that shoulder, we climbed the stairs. It took practice getting the skis positioned just right for balance and it took time to get the shoulder toughened up to deal with the weight of the skis on our bony shoulders. My right shoulder was always sore at the beginning of the winter but it didn't take long to get it in shape.

The top of the tower provided a level area large enough for 3 or 4 jumpers to place our skis down on the packed snow. The next trick involved balancing on one foot as we very carefully and thoroughly cleaned all the snow from one boot before slipping it into the binding of one ski and latching it in place. Then we balanced on the other foot to repeat the process. This could be much more difficult since we were trying to balance ourselves on a ski which would head down the hill if we were not careful to be on level snow. Occasionally, a jumper would lose control and his skis would head down the hill without him.

With skis mounted, we stood side-by-side working our way across the width of the starting platform as skier after skier took his turn. We checked and double-checked our bindings to make sure they were on properly.

One of the techniques we liked to use, if possible, to gain more speed involved placing the tail end of one ski against something solid like a wooden safety wall. With that ski secured in place, we could thrust the other ski forward. The created momentum would carry us over the front and down into the tracks.

Getting into a good in-run position as quickly as possible was crucial. In those days, a good position meant pressing our chest down against our knees, butt up so that our thighs were parallel to the skiing surface, and our arms extending down in front with the finger tips touching. (The modern day jumper rides with his arms extending to the rear.) We held that relaxed position all the way to the take off.

The take off was the most crucial moment in time. If we timed our jump perfectly, snapping both arms back and driving our bodies up and out, our ski tips would come up and we could feel the pressure of the air beneath our skis and our chests. If everything came together just perfectly, we soared through the air with arms at our sides as we extended as far as we dared over the tips of the skis.

We had to make an instantaneous decision when to back off and drop into a perfect "telemark" landing with one ski ahead of the other, knees bent, and well balanced. We held that position through the transition and onto the flat.

Stopping involved a variety of techniques depending upon the available terrain. At the Andover jump, a bit of snowplowing served the purpose. At some jumps, throwing out an anchor seemed necessary.

Getting back to the importance of timing at the takeoff, let me explain what happened when we "missed the takeoff". There were two distinct ways that one could miss the takeoff, jumping early or jumping late. Missing the takeoff would definitely cause one to have a shorter than normal jump and would most often lead to reduced style points.

Of the two misses, being early could be the most dangerous. It usually meant that the ski tips stayed down, caused by the pressure getting on top of the skis. A jack-knifed body position, bent knees, and flailing arms rescued the jumper from somersaulting. Just imagine the loss of style points!

Andover, Maine produced some of the hottest jumpers from around the state and New England and the town hall jump was probably a good reason for it. Kids had easy access to the jump located a short walk from the center of town and they jumped all hours of the day and night. The town fathers had installed lighting!

Some of my fondest memories of ski jumping involve jumping on that jump at night under the lights. As a very active member of the Pineland Ski Club, Dad made frequent trips to Andover for club meetings and we failed to miss an opportunity to use the jump under the lights.

Being a ski jumper involved looking the part. Real jumpers wore nice fitting sweaters. The classiest of the day was what I always called the Nordic sweater. It came in various colors (mostly red and navy) with a white stripe around the waist and around the neck. The neck met in a v-shape in the front and the 2-inch wide stripe followed the outline of the neck. That white vee in the front of the sweater really looked nice.

We couldn't afford such style so Mom did her best by buying some yarn and knitting ski jumping sweaters. I would have given anything for one knit just like a Nordic sweater but, instead, I settled for a bright green with white snowflakes all over. Across the chest was a wide, white, v-shaped stripe with green snowflakes. Ouch.

The Nordic hat matched the sweater in color and, when the edge was turned up, a matching white stripe circled the head. To have one of those with the matching sweater was a dream that never came true. Mom knit me a hat that matched my sweater. Oh well, at least I looked like a ski jumper.

To put the whole package together so that you truly looked like a stylish ski jumper, you wore the Nordic hat and sweater and a pair of stretch pants. They were made of some kind of durable stretchy material. They ran all the way down the ankles, held down with stretchy straps that wrapped around the bottom of the feet. Some jumpers strapped them over the bottom of the ski boots to hide the top of the boots. Oftentimes, wide suspenders under the sweater held up the pants.

Putting the whole package together gave the jumper an extra boost in style points as he stretched out over his skis in full flight. It was high school before I ever wore a pair of stretch pants.

**Tom:**

As far back as I can remember, I recall "Clancy" dressing up and heading out for the weekend ski jumping event somewhere in New England or Canada. Most often the whole family went unless the trip was too far away. One thing I will never forget about Dad's wardrobe was his ski pants.

Ski jumping consisted of far more than finding the bravado to strap big and bulky pieces of lumber to your feet and riding downhill. It was either do or die; fly through the air, land on two feet, hopefully, and follow through to the end of the outrun.

Ski jumpers were awarded points for their jumps. The first way they received points was based on distance jumped. Regardless of what happened to the jumper, distance points were determined by where his feet hit the landing hill. Whether he stood or fell mattered not. Each jumper was awarded a certain number of points taken from a chart that converted distance in feet to distance points. Obviously, if you wanted to be competitive, you had to jump as far or farther than everyone else.

The second way to compile points was according to style. Jumpers were judged for their style by a panel of 3 to 5 judges. These judges stood in a "judges' stand", strategically located to one side, and awarded each jumper points for style. Sometimes with 5 judges a high and low score were tossed out and the remaining three were added to the distance points to make up the jumper's score for that round. Two or three jumps were taken for each jumper with a combination score of the best two jumps used to determine the winner. If there were three jumps taken, the lowest score of the three jumps was tossed out.

Style in ski jumping is determined by how a jumper looks while flying through the air, pressing forward, out and over the skis, with a well-positioned body. However, it should be pointed out that over the years "style" evolved.

In the first half of the twentieth century, before ski jumping hills were designed to provide the ski jumper with a flight path that followed the contour of the landing hill – necessary to achieve maximum up hill "pressure," – jumpers style involved rotating the arms from front to back, up and over the top of the head. Therefore, a jumper earned his style point if he did all of this "stylishly" and in full control. Sounds weird, especially by today's standards.

Later on, when hill design allowed jumpers to follow the contour of the hill, being quiet with little motion, hands remaining at your side, while in steady flight was the sought after style. In addition, skis needed to be together and remain steady. Jumpers sometimes had points taken away if their skis were not perfectly parallel and floating on the same angle.

During the transition from the style of cranking the arms to the style of hands at the side, jumpers attempted a style where they stretched and held both arms out in front of them – sometimes hands together and sometimes spread apart slightly. For whatever reasons, that style died quickly. I never tried it. Probably Robert did as he is much older than I am (wink).

If you watch today's modern ski jumpers, you'll see them leave the end of the take-off and purposely spread the skis apart. They use their bodies as "foils," like the wing of an airplane. Once the technique is perfected, the jumper sails through the air to greater distances.

The judging of the jumper on style is carried throughout the jump until the jumper skis through the "transition" of the hill to the flat. He should land in a telemark landing, as Robert described earlier, always in control until the end. At that point, each judge records his points.

By now you might be asking what any of this has to do with what ski pants "Rockin' Chair Remy" wore when he jumped? By the way, Dad was tagged with the nickname, Rockin' Chair, because, when he sailed through his flight he would rock forward over his skis and then pull back a bit, then rock forward again – thus rocking chair.

It wasn't written in any judge's rule book that a ski jumper had to be wearing the very newest in fashion, but don't fool yourself if you thought it didn't matter. If you wanted to be competitive, you had to look the part of a modern day ski jumper of your era. Dad did that.

But his ski pants, his ski pants. They were gray in color and baggy, as was the style of the day. What I remember most about his White Stag ski pants, aside from the little silver "white stag" on the ends of the zippers to his pockets, was when he was flying through the air, you could hear his pants flapping in the breeze. I don't ever recall it costing him a reduction in style points. It was the fashion.

In later years, long after Dad had ended his days of competitive ski jumping, he continued to wear those same pants. Through the 1960's, when baggy and flapping ski jumping pants were well out of style, Dad's fluttering pants drew a lot of attention and prompted many a comment.

Ski clothing has evolved extensively and has become extremely expensive. After the flapping, baggy pants, came the baggy stretch pants made of a heavier material that prevented the vaunted flapping.

Now the evolution of ski jumping attire seems odd, when baggy and flapping weren't even thought of as resistant to the the wind, something that would slow a ski jumper down when speed and distance was the name of the game. In time, as that concept was considered, stretch pants evolved into a tight fitting, full body suit. That suit became thicker but lighter in weight and ultimately returned, once again, to baggy. But this time baggy became a technological issue. Suit's were being designed to assist the jumper in staying in the air longer. Much like today's "base jumping" suits, eventually restrictions had to be employed so that no jumper could gain a sudden distinct advantage.

Looking like a serious ski jumper created its own points. Dad was a competitor. He had his White Stags, green, v-neck sweater (with the white trim stripes – extremely stylish), but he seldom ever wore a hat. He wore glasses and a pair of over-the-glasses goggles with an amber lens. Accenting his attire was a pair of deer skin gloves – buckskins, he always called them. Those were his favorites. Each year he would take his deer skin fur from the deer he took during deer hunting season and trade it in for a pair of "buckskin" gloves.

*The Elm Street Jump, or more affectionately referred to as the jump behind the Town Hall in Andover, Maine. Taken during the summer months, circa 1951. - Photo courtesy of Mike Stowell.*

# The Jumping Hills

## Andover, Maine

**Robert:**

Besides the town hall jump in Andover, there were two located south of town near the old airport. Many years ago, route 5 was a slow route to travel from Rumford Point to Andover. It was much more winding and bumpy. After passing the Covered Bridge Road, it used to turn to the left passing a large, open field once used as an airport. A gravel road made its way around the airport and through young pine trees to the base of a mountain. That side of the mountain was steep and covered with ledge.

Far to the right, stood the 25 meter "high school jump". It had a natural in-run with a wooden take-off. The design was out-dated; it sent you out and suddenly down, making it difficult to hold a good flight position. Few people were interested in it. The town hall jump was a bit smaller but much more enjoyable and, if we wanted a bigger jump, the high school jump was simply not satisfactory.

The main jump at the airport was the 45-meter. It's story speaks of the passion for ski jumping that existed in the middle of the 20th century. Though the landing hill was naturally large enough for a 40 to 50 meter jump, there was not nearly enough room for a suitable in-run because of a precipitous ledge that rose well over a hundred feet into the air.

Dynamite solved the problem. That's right. They were so determined to put a ski jump on that location that they blasted the ledge away to form a flat area for a start and shaped the dynamited material into the beginnings of an in-run. Extra material helped improve the shape of the landing hill.

If that wasn't enough work, then the building of the take-off was. It was a massive wooden structure that must have been 15 feet high and 30 to 40 feet in length and 8 to 10 feet wide.

They also had to build a large, judges' tower at the side and top of the landing hill. It was built on posts. Imagine the work that was involved erecting and securing posts that would hold a small building well above a steep decline and make it solid and safe – and all with no power equipment!

Dad was instrumental in the building of that jump. He was one of the primary builders of the take-off and judges' tower. I have never forgotten the summer and fall weekends helping him carry building materials up the side of that hill.

How many sportsmen would work that hard and put that kind of effort and time into building something that could only be used a few weeks in the winter months? Many, today, would consider it ridiculous and a waste of time but, to me, it demonstrates the passion that was deep in the hearts and souls of the ski jumpers and their love of the sport.

It would be that passion that would carry the excitement and thrill of flying through the air through the 1960's and '70's. It always took commitment, passion, and hard work to provide that opportunity to our youth. Every jump that existed did so because there were people there to make it happen.

First, and foremost, a jump had to be built. Then it had to be maintained. When the snows came, the jumps had to be worked into shape. The easiest jumps to get ready were those that had a well-designed shape to them, such as the town hall jump in Andover. All of the new snow had to be packed – by foot with skis on. There were no fancy machines for grooming. The more jumpers available for packing meant less work for each of us individually but it seemed that most of the time there were only a few of us. We will cover care and maintenance later.

When we stood on the outrun of the 45-meter at the Andover airport and looked toward the mountain, we could see a wide open area to the left that ran well up the side of the mountain. We were always told that that used to be the site of a much larger jump(60+ meters). It was known as 'the man-killer'. Rumor had it that during its day a man died as a result of injuries from a fall. Anyone who may know the truth has most likely passed.

*To the right is the Andover, Maine 45-meter jumping hill located adjacent to the old airport built for possible use during World War II. Judging from the vintage cars, I would say this was in the 1950s. In what appears to be a landing hill to the left, is what remained of the "Man Killer" ski jump – perhaps an attempt to build a ski "flying" jump. There seems to be little recorded history of that jump or even how it got its nickname. - Photo courtesy of Mike Stowell.*

**Tom:**

Robert, being older (much, much older but I guess this isn't the time to bring this up), remembers more of the origins of the "Airport" jumps. I was always fascinated that this complex was commonly referred to as "The Airport." I don't remember an actual airport. For those perhaps not familiar with American history, there were similar airports elsewhere that were constructed during World War II. It was thought that airports scattered throughout strategic places in this country, might be used by American Military flight operations. Often at these airports or other strategic locations in the nearby villages, like church belfries, town hall roofs or any place where a person could stand watch, volunteers could lookout for enemy aircraft. I'm sure readers can name and locate their World War II airport that served in much the same way.

From my earliest memories of going to the Andover airport, I recall mostly the small pine trees growing up everywhere and what remained of some gravel roads. It looked like a great place to get lost.

There was also constructed at the site of the 45-meter jump, on the south side of the outrun, a relatively small, rectangular shaped building that most often was called "the warming hut." Warming huts were a bonus in those days. They were built for the jumpers to step into to get warm for a few minutes, but as I recall, they seldom used it as they stayed warm hiking up the hill for their next jump. The warming hut was a great place on cold days to watch the competition, visit with friends and perhaps get a cup of coffee or hot chocolate.

The memory of hiking up the side of the mountain to the starting area for my very first jump sticks with me well today.

The first jumpers to appear on site blazed the trail to the top of the landing hill creating steps of packed snow, sometimes immediately to the side and other times a distance away. Seldom were there any made-made steps at jumps so we trudged one step after the other through the snow. Each successive jumper tried to step into the preceding jumper's footsteps to help make the climb easier. In time the snow firmed up and "steps" were created and remained in good shape, if we could keep descending spectators or kids from wiping them out by sliding down.

The route over the second half of the climb depended upon the construction of the jump. If it was a tower, steps were built up one side. For the 45-meter jump in Andover, the steps to the top were through the woods and to the left as you might face the jump from the parking area.

As I worked my way for the first time up the mountain, I joined the end of a line of jumpers. The dynamited start area comfortably allowed several jumpers, maybe 10 or more, the room to prepare and get themselves properly into their skis. As each jumper left the start, the remaining jumpers shuffled to their left making room for the next jumper to get ready.

I first realized that this start area had been blasted away thanks to my Uncle Stan Remington. When I made a comment about the starting area, he said, "We blasted all this ledge out of here." I really don't know who he meant by "we", but I'm sure that most, if not all, were members of the Pineland Ski Club.

The names of people that I can remember who were heavily involved with the club, skiing and ski jumping, are Paul, Alan, and Jim Bodwell, David and John Percival, Clarence and Stanley Remington, Hoppy Morgan, Roger Mills, Learned Littlehale, the

Marston's, the Akers and the list could go on and on. Oh my, and who have I forgotten?

The construction of jumping sites, maintaining them and organizing events was, almost always, done by volunteers. God bless them. The bigger jumps, like the 45-meter jump in Andover, were seldom brought into shape early in the season and kept that way throughout the winter season. It was just too much work unless a group of jumpers were going to use it on a regular basis.

The 45 meter jump was never put in shape until days before the annual Winter Carnival, usually in March, in time to get in some practice jumps. Sometimes weather would prohibit early practices. Either way, the volunteers always pulled off a great carnival, with several skiing events for all ages, bringing together many people and their families.

**Robert:**

Ski jumping in soft snow was extremely dangerous. For this reason, we spent the first opportunity after a snow storm packing and shaping the jump. A very cold night following this was often necessary to allow the packed snow the chance to firm up. After significant snowfall, a foot or more, we prepared the jump differently than for smaller storms.

The landing hill had to be firm. The method used depended more upon the need for the snow and the desire to jump. If there was an ample base of snow on the hill and we wanted to jump that day, we carried our skis to the top of the landing hill and began the process of side-slipping down the hill to push the new snow to the bottom where we would man snow shovels and remove the snow. We usually left an inch or two behind so that we could pack it into the old snow that was beneath.

If we needed the snow because there wasn't a good base, the process usually began by putting our skis on at the bottom and side packing up the hill. Once we made it to the top of the landing hill, we worked our way back down the hill using short, choppy steps trying very carefully to leave a well-groomed packed surface without pushing any snow down the hill. This often meant that the hill was too soft to jump on.

In the event of a large accumulation of heavy, wet snow, the preferred method was "boot packing". Everyone removed his skis and climbed onto the hill to take part in the tedious process of packing the snow down with boots. Boot packing in these types of snow conditions was necessary to avoid the very dangerous situation that would arise if we packed with our skis. Packing deep, wet snow with skis only served to pack the top few inches leaving unpacked, soft snow beneath. This would create a "crust" which jumpers, in time, would break through causing a potentially dangerous and injurious fall.

Packing the out-run was definitely a time-consuming process. We had to pack it wide enough to allow for the possibility of a fall. If a jumper fell, he often ended up sliding down the hill and off to the side. Coming to a sudden stop in unpacked powder could easily lead to broken bones. The out-run also had to be packed long enough to allow each jumper ample opportunity to stop safely.

Similar techniques were used on the in-run. Whether we packed up then down or just down, depended upon the need for the new snow and/or our desire to jump that day.

If conditions were too soft for jumping, we rode down the landing hill on our skis, being careful to ride in different paths to avoid putting in any ski ruts that might freeze over night.

Once the hill was ready to be used, the task of "setting tracks" usually fell on the shoulders of the most experienced. The very first person to use the jump after the hill was prepared had to do it with no ski tracks in the in-run. He had to carefully plan and line up his path down the in-run and off the takeoff, leaving behind a perfectly spaced pair of parallel tracks for the next jumper to follow. His concern was not how well or how far he jumped but rather the quality of the tracks he left behind. As each jumper took his turn, the tracks would begin to wear in and get faster and, in time, each jumper's concentration turned from the tracks to the quality of his jump.

Jumping the first day after a storm was not usually very enjoyable since new snow was slow and good jumps were difficult to achieve. As the days went by after a storm, the snow got older and faster and jumping was awesome. Sometimes, conditions got so fast that we were jumping to unsafe distances.

The remedy for this depended upon the jump. If the jump allowed for the option of lowering the starting point, the speed that jumpers could attain would be reduced, resulting in shorter, safer jumps. Most jumps did not have that option so we "cut the takeoff". Someone would climb onto the end of the takeoff and use a snow shovel to chop off the end a designated distance - more of a guess than anything else.

On practice days when a wide range in the abilities of the jumpers existed, cutting the takeoff made it difficult for the weaker jumpers to reach the landing hill. On such days, the better jumpers could stand erect with their arms extended wide on their way down the top of the in-run to reduce their speed.

On competition day, the longest jumper determined the need for cutting the takeoff. Sometimes this created controversy. When I was on the ski team at UMaine, Orono, the University of Vermont had two Norwegian jumpers on their team. One was a big, strapping fellow by the name of Petr Kongsli. Kongsli possessed an incredible vertical leap with thighs as big around as my waist. The other Norwegian on their team was sort of a test pilot. The competition officials used his practice rides to decide how far to cut the takeoff to make it safe for Mr. Kongsli. By the time the competition began, the takeoff had been cut so far back that getting onto the landing hill was a major accomplishment for most of us.

*An outstanding photograph depicting the near perfect style of Robert Remington*

The last competition of my jumping career took place at St. Lawrence University and, for some reason, the officials refused to cut the takeoff, making it possible to get in good rides. Meanwhile, Petr Kongsli out-jumped the hill. He landed so far down onto flat ground that his legs weren't strong enough and he fell down on every jump. A fall is a 10 point deduction in style points from each judge! For the first time, he didn't win! He placed second behind his Norwegian countryman.

In modern times this is dealt with in major competitions by allowing the jumpers to select different starting positions and their points are adjusted accordingly by a predetermined method.

**Tom:**

The Andover Winter Carnival was one of a few major winter skiing events held in Maine. Typically it took place at the end of February or early March and was hosted by the Pineland Ski Club.

I recently discovered an archived copy of a newspaper article from the Lewiston Daily Sun (now the Sun Journal) dated December 7, 1940 – exactly one year prior to the bombing of Pearl Harbor that drew America into the World War in the Pacific Theater.

The article read:

*"Andover – At the first meeting of the Pineland Ski Club this Fall to prepare for the Winter's program of sports, new officers for the coming year were elected. Merton Fox, was again elected to head the organization with Robert B. Swain as vice president; W. E. Merrill, secretary; Herbert Hall, treasurer. No action was taken concerning the annual Northern New England Ski Championships and carnival otherwise than to set the dates as*

*March, 1, 2, and for Classes A. B. and C.* [This is exactly as it appears in the newspaper] *Carnival committees will be elected at a later meeting. A membership drive has netted 178 members to the Pineland club.*

*Skiing conditions are excellent at Andover with five inches new powder on 20 inches of base. All trails open, slopes excellent and the junior jump at the slalom slope is in use."*

Imagine back in 1940 a membership drive in a Maine town of 757 people recruiting 178 new members. I doubt that today anyone could recruit that many people within a population center of over one million. But, that's the way it was back then and the results speak for themselves.

I remember vividly the nighttime ski jumping exhibition. There were no electric lights on the Andover 45-meter jump but it didn't matter. A large, flaming hoop, several feet in diameter stood at the end of the take-off and torches lined the in-run and landing hill. Jumpers willing to risk their necks, carried a torch in each hand as they went off the jump. The crowd loved it and showed their appreciation after each jumper with a lengthy "applause" that came from car horns in the parking lot.

An additional attraction called for two jumpers coming off the jump at the same time, side by side. A variation of that would find one jumper following directly behind the other. Daring they were and didn't they love their sport!

The Carnival was a smash hit. I remember entering some of the competitions. There were cross-country ski races for all ages. Often I, and other kids just like me, skied four events on the same pair of skis, all in one day. I think cross-country went first, early in the morning. At the conclusion of that event, we moved over to the slalom slope and had a try at that. In the afternoon, we wrapped things up with a jumping event at the jump behind the town hall.

The big hill jumping event, sometimes the Northern New England ski jumping championships took place on Sunday. Ski jumpers from all over the northeast and Canada would come to compete. Days before the event, the Town of Andover used their big plow trucks to open the access road and clear the parking area. The jumping hill had been groomed to top form and decorated with banners of red, white, and blue. This was all topped off with wiring up a public address system so that announcers could keep spectators informed and introduce each jumper by name and announce distance jumped.

While spectators were waiting for the event to begin and competitors were taking practice jumps, Sousa Marches echoed from the PA system. I fell in love with Sousa marches. Even to this day, when I hear a Sousa march playing, my mind immediately rushes back to the days of ski jumping competitions in the late 1950s and into the 1960s.

After the competition was complete, everyone drove back to the town hall and waited for results. I was fascinated by the idea that, as each competitor received his trophy at the front of the room, he was expected to kiss the Carnival Queen – SCANDALOUS!

Winter carnivals were big in New England and Andover happened to be only one of the many sponsoring towns.

## Rumford, Maine

**Robert:**

Winter Carnivals were definitely popular when we were kids and the Rumford version sponsored by the Chisholm Ski Club was one of the best. Prior to 1960, Scotty's Mountain was the location of three ski jumps. These were called the grammar school jump, the high school jump, and Suicide Hill. As kids, we used the grammar and high school jumps but never the 55-meter Suicide jump. I remember watching some exciting competition on the 55. It had a long, natural landing hill and the takeoff and in-run were on a tower that rose above the surrounding pines. The Chisholm Ski Club also used this jump for night jumping through a ring of fire.

Scotty's was on land owned by Scotty Richardson right behind where Mt. Valley High School is located today. I have often wondered how great it would be for the Mt. Valley kids to be able to go right behind the school for jumping. Oh, that's right, no jumping since .....?

*Scotty's Mountain, Rumford, Maine. "Suicide Hill" it was often called. Why? I'm not really sure. This was a great jumping venue for many years. - Photo courtesy of Richard Kent.*

It was about 1960 that Black Mountain opened and skiing at Scotty's either ended abruptly or slowly faded away. I don't recall. I do know that by the time we were old enough to jump on the 55-meter, we were no longer going to Scotty's. I'm guessing because the hill had closed and all jumping was in full swing at Black Mountain.

*The Aurele Legere Jump located at Black Mountain in Rumford, Maine. Perhaps not an architect's dream design, but it didn't curb the enthusiasm that once was on display for ski jumping. - Photo courtesy of Richard Kent.*

## Bethel, Maine

From the time we were very young through our high school years, we spent more time jumping at the Swans Corner jumps on the Sunday River Road than all other venues combined. At one time, there were as many as four jumps at Swans though I don't believe they were ever in jumping shape at the same time. From left to right across the slope were a 10-meter, a 45-meter, a 30-meter, and a 20-meter.

By the time we were ready to jump on the 30 – and we were actually pretty young – the 30 and 45 were the only ones we used. The smaller jumps were used for beginning jumpers and my father worked very hard to get beginners ready for the 30 - probably so we wouldn't have to take care of the smaller jumpers.

The area at Swans was used by the Gould Academy ski teams. The area to the left of the 45, as you looked up the hill, was open and groomed by skiers for alpine skiing prior to the opening of Sunday River Skiway. One source has the area opening around 1945 with a rope tow added in 1950. The tow was used by the alpine skiers and the jumpers. Since Sunday River opened in 1959, when I was 11 years old, the use of the Swans area for alpine was nearly over by the time we were using the jumps on a regular basis. So, by the early '60's, the alpine skiers were gone but the rope tow was still there and usable.

The tow line ran up the left side of the 30-meter jump, powered by a gasoline-powered engine. The rope traveled down the slope along automobile wheels attached to utility poles. Once the Gould ski team brought the rope from storage and attached it to the tow each winter, all we had to do was provide the gasoline and hope we could get the engine started. It did not like the cold weather.

The days that we managed to get it running were unbelievable! Instead of taking our skis off at the end of a jump and carrying them all the way to the top, we could ski over to the rope tow and ride to the top.

Getting off the lift was a bit difficult. The long, heavy jumping skis on our feet along with the fact that we had to unload while on the up-slope made it a major challenge to get off the rope without falling, getting tangled in the rope, or snapping the rope enough that it came off its track. But, once we got the hang of it, we could ski a short distance to the base of the start tower, take off our skis, and climb to the starting platform. We were easily able to get in 3 to 5 times as many jumps in whatever time we had available.

**Tom:**

I know little of the history of ski jumping at Black Mountain, although I did compete and train on all of the jumps. I enjoyed the two bigger hills the most. I do recall one time traveling to Black Mountain to train with the Gould Academy ski team and Eric Roderick, from the Rumford High School ski team joined us. It gave us a chance to get to know one another a little bit.

According to Rich Kent's book, *Words for a Mountain*, Black Mountain opened in 1962. I was only 9 years old when the site was under construction and I remember it well.

One summer day, Peter Davis, a ski jumper of the time, showed up at our house driving a Model T Ford. Dad rode "shotgun" and my brother Alan and I rode in the Rumble Seat. What a blast! We traveled to the Black Mountain site and saw the lodge and some of the ski trails under construction. I don't, however, recall, that any of the jumps were yet being built...but they may have been.

My earliest recollection of the existence of the Swan's Corner/Gould Academy facility was at an age where most of my skiing and ski jumping was off the snowbanks in East Bethel. But I do remember spending time as a "little shaver" in the warming hut at the bottom of the 30-meter hill and making a nuisance of myself sliding down the side of the hill. The hut had a double barreled wood stove in it and when it really got fired up, it often caused inhabitants to open the doors (one at each end) to cool it off. There was a period of time when vandals took out some of the glass in the big windows of the hut that faced the jumping hill. Eventually those were repaired, I assume by Gould Academy.

When Dad wasn't away at a ski jumping competition, he spent at least every Sunday afternoon at Swan's and sometimes Saturday's. Often the Saturdays were taken up by a Gould Academy or, later on, a Telstar High School ski jumping competition.

It must have been early to mid 1960s that I "got into" ski jumping. I think the transition for ski jumpers from hill rider to ski jumper comes once the bravado appears that prompts a jumper to trust the air pressure hitting him in the face. Hill riding was really nothing but work: climb up the hill, slide down the hill and be airborne for a short period of time, maintaining balance to the end and then doing it all over again. Nothing changed. Fun but boring.

*Tom Remington, circa 1966, looking a bit nervous, perhaps contemplative. A youngster at Gould Academy, I'm sure he was sizing up the stiff competition that awaited.*

It was common practice for a jumper to ride the landing hill once, and more if that's what it took, to get up the courage. I usually did that throughout my jumping career when I visited a jump for the first time, or if conditions were sketchy.

However, once a jumper discovers the thrill of "flying" through the air and the combination of looking for more speed, jumping harder, and pressing toward the tips of his skis, the boredom of hill riding morphed into the thrill of flying. Once this transition happens, where a ski jumper goes from there, is really dependent on many things, one being the insatiable lust for more, faster, farther, longer....competition.

I am going to back up for just a bit here and discuss equipment again. Skiing in the front and back yard at home could be accomplished with a concoction of about anything you could get fixed onto you feet. Probably readers already got a sense of that from reading the earlier accounts of equipment and clothing. But, when we graduated to the bigger hills, the need for better and bigger skis and boots grew.

As I have pointed out before, Dad was good at scrounging up skis and boots from somewhere. They were usually old and hand-me-downs, or perhaps even a pair of jumping skis that suffered a break. A trip to Henry Paradis in South Paris could cure the break and another pair of skis was available to share.

Since I was the youngest of four boys, I became accustomed to getting everything my three older brothers had used, including boots and clothing. We attended Gould Academy in Bethel. Sonny and Robert each attended Gould for four years. Al and I attended 3 and 2 years, respectively, before Telstar High School opened in the fall of 1968.

As each brother entered Gould, the ski team provided jumping skis and sometimes boots, removing one more from the family pool of skiers needing jumping skis. I moved up to something bigger and better each year until the day that I entered Gould Academy and got a quality pair of skis. (Note: In reality, through the generosity of Gould Academy, I was provided with my first pair of quality jumping skies. I was in eighth grade.)

Along with the transition from hill rider to ski jumper, better skis only contributed to the thrill of it all. Swan's Corner was the training ground for many a ski jumper from the Bethel region and/or Gould Academy and Telstar High Schools.

*Swan's Corner jumping competition – Telstar High School versus other schools, circa 1970. Here Tom Remington leaves the end of the take off looking to stretch out and level off the skis for a long flight down the hill.*

**Robert:**

Working on a project like this has afforded me the opportunity to

54

spend time reminiscing and it daily amazes me what literally pops into my head. Earlier today a Facebook posting of a picture of Alan, Tony, Howard, and Sammy Chapman, who grew up on the Northwest Bethel Road, reminded me of spending time at their home which was situated on the side of a hill where we did some "backyard skiing".

The picture also reminded me that Alan, who was the oldest of the four brothers in the picture, developed a passion for the sport of ski jumping that probably surpassed the passion of the Remington boys. I remember his eagerness to listen and learn from Dad as we spent countless hours at the Swan's Corner jumps.

There were many Bethel area boys who benefited from Dad's tutelage and enthusiasm. He would help anyone even if it meant that they would become better ski jumpers than his own sons; that happened often.

We lived about six miles from town and, every time we went to town, we had to pass the home of one of the best local jumpers that I remember. We took him with us to the Swan's jumps nearly every time we went. He was the aforementioned Peter Davis, a few years older than me, and I have never forgotten how good he was. He became a role model for kids my age. The kid could fly. He would repeatedly do what Tom described above. He was after speed and distance. He would lay out over the tips of his skis and he seemed to stretch his body, extending his chin out to ride the air nearly to the bottom of the hill. He was tough to beat.

Once Peter Davis moved on, along came Greg Howe. Greg took over the role of the one we wanted to emulate. Greg traveled with us everywhere we went.

The best jump at the Swan's Corner facility was the 45-meter. The sad thing is that it was a jump that didn't get used a lot. It had some design flaws. Two of these flaws could only be overcome by lots of snow and work. The take off was too low and it sat too far back from the landing hill. That meant shoveling tons of snow onto the take off, building it up to a height that would get us over the knoll and onto the landing hill.

If that wasn't enough work, the landing hill had a big sag in it about halfway down and we had to shovel snow into it to get it built up enough to be able to groom the hill into nice shape.

The third flaw was easy to deal with. There was no starting tower so we simply hiked back up the slope to a point that would give us the speed we needed. It meant a very long ride on the in-run. It also meant a very long walk to get back to the top for a ride.

The work and the walk were worth it. Once the 45 was in shape, we hated going back to the 30. The uniqueness of the ride off that 45 occurred right after take off. The distance from the end of the take off to the knoll where the landing hill began was longer than normal. When we took off and started to press out over our skis, there was an usually long delay before the landing slope came into view. But, when it did, what a feeling! There was an extra rush of pressure against the body and skis and we could extend and press out and down the hill. We could get good, long rides of 120 to 150 feet. It always seemed that we were in the air a very long time.

**Tom:**

The 45-meter jump was my favorite of many jumps in Maine but it was unfortunate that it was seldom open for jumping.

One winter day, the 30-meter and 45-meter jumps were open at the same time. There was a path that ran along the side of the mountain between the top of the landing hills of the two jumps –

you did have to cross the rope tow line along the way.

I took a couple of jumps on the 30-meter and then moved over to the 45 to jump. I really enjoyed that hill but I wasn't as comfortable on the bigger hill when I was trying to work on things I needed to improve. So, I went back to the 30-meter and practiced, then returned to the 45. I took advantage of a rare opportunity.

Most of my Sunday afternoons throughout high school were spent at Swan's Corner. We would toss our jumping skis into the back of Clancy's 1956 Ford pickup truck with homemade dual stacks and head for the jump, stopping to pick up any other interested jumpers like Larry Fox, along the way. Larry's father, Stan, and my father competed in ski jumping during their high school years in Andover and it was Larry's grandfather, Merton Fox, who was one of those in the early years involved in Andover skiing and the Pineland Ski Club.

Mike Bates was a local boy and a ski jumper on the Gould Academy Ski Team - so local that he lived in a house right beside the outrun of the 30-meter jump.

*Swan's Corner jumping competition. This photo gives a good representation of the hill, the crowds, the judges' stand, the Sunday River Rd. and the attention from passersby to the activity. Here a jumper soars past the stand as the judges look on preparing to score the competitor. As an FYI, the gentleman in the judges' stand nearest us and leaning hard for the jumper, is Clarence "Rockin' Chair" Remington.*

There were others from out of town who might appear on a Sunday afternoon for jumping practice: Mike Mickericz from Rumford, George Perry from Mexico, perhaps some or all of the Broomhalls from the Rumford and Mexico area, the Rodericks, Millers, Rosses and many, many more.

When I was a sophomore at Gould Academy, the school brought to the town a big name in American ski jumping – Art Tokle, Sr. We all went to the Swan's Corner jump where he conducted a clinic for all the jumpers on the Gould jumping team. What an event and one that was made possible through the generosity of Gould and the simple fact that there was a skiing complex right nearby. It was a distinct advantage to attend a school with skiing facilities at easy access and to bring in people like Art Tokle and others to give clinics.

A little note of interest: At that time, I was pretty cocky and carried a pretty big chip on my shoulder. I had competed for Gould in ski jumping as an eighth-grader (legal then?) and thought I was God's gift to Gould Academy and the world of ski jumping. I thought that I was going to impress Mr. Tokle. I guess I did. He never spoke to me until after my third or fourth jump. As I crested the top of the landing hill, he stood in the judge's stand looking away from me. I looked at him, waiting to make eye contact, and asked him what he thought of my jump. I don't remember his exact words but I got his message. When I was ready to actually put some effort into what I was doing, he would be willing to put some effort into coaching me. What the heck did he know? He read *me* like a book.

## Ups and Downs

**Robert:**

Since Tom has introduced the telling of personal stories, I shall take this opportunity to tell one of my own. As previously mentioned, the task of carrying long, heavy jumping skis was a necessary skill to learn. After the completion of a jump and coming to a stop at the end of the outrun, the jumper would, if possible, ski back to the base and side of the landing hill by skating. Think about that concept for awhile and you'll begin to realize that it could be quite an accomplishment. Getting started was the most difficult but, with three or four forceful thrust off alternating skis, we could gain enough speed to skate back along the side of the outrun and remove our skis at the base of the climb.

On the Swan's 30-meter hill the climb was on the right side of the hill as you looked up. A winding, foot-trodden path made it's way to the top of the landing hill. From there to the base of the starting tower the path was much straighter and not nearly as steep. Keeping in mind that these long, heavy skis were balanced on one shoulder and add to that the fact that the sole of our boots was leather and your experience with what happens to snow when it is repeatedly packed and you can imagine just how slippery, and therefore, treacherous walking around with skis on your shoulder could be.

Despite all I knew about the art of carrying skis under these conditions, one day I learned a lesson the hard way. I had just begun my climb from the top of the landing hill and was moving along the side of the takeoff when someone from behind called my name. I stopped and spun around. Both feet slipped out from under me and I landed with the full weight of my body and the skis right on my tail bone. The injury ended my skiing for that day and several days following.

As if the ensuing pain wasn't enough, the embarrassment of having everyone look at me in "that" way was too much. You wonder what I mean by "that" way? It's quite difficult for me to find the appropriate words so I will trust that most readers either have had the experience personally or have witnessed others experience how one walks when he or she has soiled the britches. You get the picture now?

But with the bad comes the good. I learned through that experience and not just the obvious, don't-walk-downhill-while-carrying-skis. I learned that the tailbone is called the coccyx and it is the triangular bony structure at the base of the vertebral column and the condition is called coccydynia, Latin for "I messed my pants"? I took two years of Latin in high school and minored in biology in college. How wonderful that things work together so well!

Each day that I sit down to write I am never sure just what I'm about to write. It usually is something that comes to mind after I read what Tom has written. Other times it's simply what "pops to mind". Since you have read to this point, you probably have a good idea by now that our writing is not some work that we carefully and methodically plotted in advance.

Before starting this project, we agreed that our purpose was to try to give readers a "feel for what skiing, and particularly ski jumping, was like during our times." Since part of that time was the reality that all that we did was not part of a well-designed master plan and we operated day-to-day looking for fun, such is the style of this project.

To this point, I wish now to tell you that ski jumping is still in my soul at the age of 66. Yes, it is and I can prove it by relating two facts. First is the manner in which I watch ski jumping on television. When ski jumping is broadcast, the camera angle is always from one side of the hill. This past Olympics, for example, showed the jumpers moving from right to left across the screen. It never fails that at some point in the coverage I discover that I am "jumping" with each jumper. That is, my body involuntarily "snaps" at the takeoff and leans in the direction he or she is moving. It's not until the jumper lands that I realize that I'm leaning to one side. I sit up straight and think, "Stop it," but I can't.

Okay, now for fact number two and I hesitate to relate this for fear of suggestions that I seek counseling. I have had recurring dreams my whole adult life. Though the dreams vary in nature and location, they all have the same foundation. In those dreams, I have the ability to run and jump off cliffs, high buildings, and mountains. As soon as I'm airborne, I assume a perfect ski jumping flight position and safely float to the ground. What a ride! Okay bring on the shrinks.

**Tom:**

Respice ad me! Sum! Look at me! I'm flying! I don't think I'll touch that one. I won't even tell you what somebody told me once about what dream flying means. However, a "Google Fu" (a quick search of the Internet) tells me that dreams of flying are a good thing and the dreamer usually awakens the next morning feeling pretty darn good. (Also makes him feel like he has set new hill records.)

And, I would be lying if I said I hadn't had the same experience. So, my question is this: Because I feel so good, is it why I became a ski jumper, or, because I am a ski jumper I dream, therefore I feel good? Let's move on.

In case you hadn't figured it out yet, maintaining a ski jump takes a lot of work. The bigger the jump the bigger the effort required to keep it up. Ski jumping, at least in Maine, died an agonizing and sputtering death, mostly due to ridiculous insurance rates. I've always been perplexed over this conundrum. Some of us have laid some of the blame on the American Broadcasting Company's repeated portrayal in the opening segment of Wide World of Sports, where a Yugoslavian jumper named Vinko Bogataj, falls on his approach to the end of the take-off, during a "ski flying" event in Oberstdorf, West Germany. It seems that ABC "spanned the globe to bring us the constant variety of sports" and the best they could come up with was this event, in which the skier was not hurt, and the weekly drumming of "the agony of defeat" brainwashed Americans and, in particular, the insurance companies.

My disarray comes many years later. I tired of hearing people speak about ski jumping only in terms of "the agony of defeat" for one Vinko Bogataj. I don't think it was ABC's intention to brainwash the masses of people to a point of framing ski jumpers as part of some kind of dystopian community of thrill seekers. And yet, "Extreme Sports" fascinate our society today. Even at the height of my "dare devilry" days, when I would have been eager to jump out of a perfectly good airplane, I'm not sure I would have attempted some of the "Extreme Sports" of today. So, what gives with the insurance? And is ski jumping not thrilling enough? Can this ever be fixed?

Due to increases in insurance, the costs associated with meeting regulatory standards of ski jumping facilities, reached unsustainable levels forcing high schools and colleges to abandon the jumps and the sport.

Because ski jumps required so much work, only those willing to put the effort into a quality facility were the last to go. With a seriously reduced availability to jumping facilities, interest and level of competition began to drop.

The maintenance effort was tiring and time consuming. My father was a nut, of sorts, when it came to taking care of a ski jump. The countless Sunday afternoons spent at Swan's Corner were memorable and one of the memories was what took place after a wonderful and fun day of ski jumping – leaving the jumping hill in perfect condition for the next time.

All jumpers reported to the top of the landing hill with jumping skis. We packed, side slipped, or whatever was needed to bring the landing hill smooth and flat – meaning no sags, gullies, humps or bumps. Often Dad would man the snow shovel. He would toss snow into areas that needed to be filled and we packed and smoothed the hill leaving it a perfect ride.

Usually when we returned the next time - sometimes it was the next day - the hill was ready and perfect. We left it that way each time. It was drummed into our heads.

At times snow was scarce. Snow shovelers would have to travel into the woods, away from the hill, to find snow. Sometimes peach baskets, garbage cans, boxes or anything that would hold snow was used.

I recall one year there was no snow – not even enough to scrape up to cover anything. We had a heavy rainstorm and the field at Swan's Corner, that was part of the outrun, flooded and then froze like a big skating rink.

A few days later we had a very small snow event leaving barely enough snow to cover the grass. The wind blew most of it into drifts near the woods at the end of the field. Over several days, our ski team went to the jump after school to haul snow. We brought boxes, shovels, cans, etc. We found snow wherever it was and began covering just enough of the in-run, take-off and landing hill to make it usable. The real problem became the skating rink-like outrun. Whatever snow fell or we put on there would blow off. The only cure was either mother nature or humans put enough snow on the ice so it wouldn't blow all away.

By this time we were going to the jump after school and at night after supper. Volunteers came with pick-up trucks, some with plows and some without. We plowed, hauled and even used snow blowers to move snow onto the ice. With a lot of effort, blood, sweat and tears, the jump became usable. It was perhaps the only ski jump that could be used in much of the state.

As interest in the sport decreased, the chances of finding people willing to work that hard to ready a ski jump became few and far between. Everything seemed to diminish toward the end of a fabulous sport.

**Robert:**

Since we are on the topic of the death of ski jumping in Maine, let me add to Tom's viewpoint. Maine ski jumping remained strong through the late 1970's. By that time, I was no longer competing and, in fact, I gave it up all together. But, I remained involved as a coach at Telstar and ski jumping at the high school level showed no signs of fading.

Things began to change in the early 1980's. Tom has already mentioned the major increase in insurance and the effect of "the agony of defeat" clip shown repeatedly on Wide World of Sports, but there were other issues that added to this spike in insurance costs. Without going into detail and naming parties involved, let me simply say that human error or poor judgment had something to do with it.

Passion for the sport may have actually added to this. The desire of competition organizers to pull off events combined with jumpers passion to compete may have prompted poor decision making. Sometimes jumps were opened when they weren't safe. Injuries resulted, some of which were severe.

This all happened at a time when we had two winters in a stretch of three years with very little snow. During one of those years we were still playing soccer on bare ground in February. It was just simply too much. As we have said before, it took a tremendous amount of work from some very dedicated people to keep a jump in shape for the winter. Every jump had at least one person who was the impetus behind its remaining in shape.

Besides the jump at Swan's Corner, high schools could depend on Black Mt. and the folks of the Chisholm Ski Club, the jump at Titcomb Mt. in Farmington and I'm sure Galen Sayward had a lot to do with that. There were also Pettengil Park in Auburn, Lost Valley in Auburn, Starks in Fryeburg, and Livermore Falls had a very nice 30-meter that was fairly new. Kents Hill had a jump next to their ski slope that I remember being used at least until the late '70's. These are all that I can remember that were usable by the late '70's and early '80's. With all these issues at hand at the same time, the Maine Principals Association dropped ski jumping after the '81 season. The last state meet was held at the Kancamagus jump in Conway, NH in 1981.

Jumping was revived briefly in the mid '90's when Bill Clough, John Wight, and Paul McGuire at Gould Academy convinced Don Angevine to redesign the 30 meter. Local volunteers, like Sonny Hastings and Dick Douglass, donated time, equipment , and materials to rebuild the hill to modern specifications. Insurance was available on a day-of-use basis only and the Gould team competed throughout New England.

Anyone who skied during the era of jumping as one of the four events – the others being, slalom, giant slalom, and x-c – will remember that jumping was often the event that determined the overall 4-event champion. Without a good jumping team, a school had little hope of being anything but an also-ran.

I attended Gould Academy from 1964 to 1967. According to the

Maine Principals Association website, in '64 and '65 there were two classes for high school skiing, 'A' and 'B'. Rumford High School claimed the State 'A' title in '64 and Edward Little in '65. In '66, the MPA added a third class, 'AA'. Edward Little captured the 'AA' crown in '66 and Gould came away with it in '67 (I don't think this is accurate).

In those days, scoring was based on a percent-behind system. The best four skiers' scores or times were added to form a 'base'. Each team's best four scores or times were added to form a team total. In jumping, the team total was divided by the 'base' and converted to a percent to determine the team score. The closer a team was to 100% the better. Good jumping teams often finished above 95% with others falling far behind. The point spread in the jumping event was often a huge determining factor.

Also consider the following. In the other events, fastest time was the goal. The four fastest times were added to form the 'base'. The team time was the sum of the team's best four finishers' times. Now, instead of dividing the team time by the 'base' (which was *lower*), the 'base' had to be divided by the team time. Therefore, teams' percent scores were much closer to each other. A team finishing fifth, for example, in the timed events could easily have a score in the 90's whereas in jumping the fifth place might easily score less than 80. (I hope I have made that math easy enough for the reader to follow.)

By the time coaches began to realize and complain about this, ski jumping went away as the scoring method changed to the points-by-finish-place method. In fact, once jumping was no longer a sanctioned event, the percent-back method for the other 'timed' events would have been a 'fair' method. The percent-back method was definitely more time consuming in the days before computer technology. All computations were done by hand with paper and pencil(no calculators either). Waiting for results literally took hours.

One could easily argue that, in this day of computers and the speed at which all can be calculated and communicated, schools should return to the percent-back system for it is a truer demonstration of the goal of those sports – time and the differences between skiers. Using this method would, in fact, guarantee that the team with the fastest combined *time* would be the winner. Not necessarily so with the points-by-place method.

## Other Jumps

**Tom:**

Early on in this account, we both spent some time describing how our back and front yards became the sites for numerous snow related activities. It was a huge winter playground and wonderland and contributed to our successes in years to come as competitors.

But we didn't own an exclusive right to backyard ski jumps or downhill courses. Once upon a time, kids played outside and humps and bumps and jumps were a common thing - not only in rural settings but in urban regions as well.

We used to visit friends and use a small jump that was constructed on the side of a hill in the area known as Virginia – a small settlement on U.S. Route 2 heading west out of Rumford. A prime example of a neighborhood jump or a back yard playground, it was somewhere on the north side of Prospect Avenue. Perhaps it's the same jump that Rich Kent mentions on page 60 of his book, *Words for a Mountain*. If you have yet to get a copy of that book, I encourage you to do so. It is a wonderful tribute to Black Mountain. There are some great pictures and writings that will zap your memory.

*From the top looking down at the West Paris "back yard" jump just off High Street –*
*Photo courtesy of Gary Inman, circa 1968*

I never had the distinct pleasure or, perhaps more accurately, the opportunity - to take my life into my hands and jump on the ski jump on High Street in West Paris. The Inmans were the proud managers and architects of that project. I can only be thankful that I never received an invitation. The stories alone scare the daylight out of me and invoke nervous giggles.

I would like to share some memories of places that I knew of either as an alpine or cross country skier, a jumper, or a meet official. I will throw out some names and locations in Maine and New England where ski jumping events took place.

There was a small ski jump on the side hill next to the upper athletic field at Gould Academy. A small tower built from wood provided a start. The landing hill was sufficient but it seemed you had to continue downhill until you reached Lover's Lane to be able to stop. (Note: If Freshman Brook wasn't iced over, you ran the risk of getting wet – or worse.) It would have taken less time getting back to the top of the hill had I taken a bus.

Rumford Point had a jump on the side hill to the north side of the village behind the fire station and it was lighted for night jumping.

When I was in high school, we competed regularly with Oxford Hills High School. They really never had a good jumping facility but were always competitive. I have to mention that during a short period of time, perhaps around 1968 or 1969, we traveled to Hebron. I was going to say to get there we drove "down the back way" but then realized the only way to Hebron is "down the back way." We turned left and ended up in a place called Fertile Valley. I'm not even going to wager a guess as to how that name came about.

At least three events were undertaken there: slalom, giant slalom and cross country. I believe it was there that Oxford Hills ski team shook our bus quite vigorously while we were trying to wax for the cross country event. We got back at them by setting a fire extinguisher loose and tossing it onto the bus. Oh, the fun. (Note: During the alpine ski events this day at Fertile Valley, Bud Howe took movies and photographs of most of the Telstar competitors. Where those films are today, I don't know. It's also where Bobby

Howe got his nickname "Hollywood." Movies? Hollywood? You get it?

Robert has mentioned Pettingill Park ski jump in Auburn. That was the site of my last official ski jumping competition and my biggest competitor in my class that day was Judd Strunk – think "A Daisy a Day."

Lost Valley ski jump could have been a better jump than it was. The outrun was too short and I remember one event when a fellow teammate fell at the bottom of the hill. His ski came off and not only did the ski not stop, it appeared to accelerate. When it hit the snow bank, the ski launched at the perfect angle so that the ski entered the front door window on the passenger's side of a car and exited the driver's side window. Perhaps the windows were rolled down? Or not!

This jump lacked a good level starting place. During one event we had to hang onto a rope until we could get our skis headed in a downhill direction. As one of the last jumpers, I had a distinct disadvantage because by the time I got to my final jump, the rope had stretched out so much that I was losing speed by starting at least 5 feet lower than the first round.

I honestly don't know if the jump I competed at once in Fryeburg was named Starks or not. I think it was located behind some municipal buildings just before the New Hampshire state line. I never jumped so hard just to make the top of the landing hill. But, that's where everybody landed. I don't believe jumping distances varied by 3 feet. Most points were given to the one who could grunt the loudest. I came away with a sore throat.

Jumping over to New Hampshire, I remember competing on at least two jumps. In Conway there was a jump on the left side of the

Kancamagus Highway heading north.

When I attended Gould Academy, we traveled to Holderness, New Hampshire. I enjoyed their ski jump. The setting was a good one for both competitors and spectators. What I remember most about the jump is that, if you were strong enough and brave enough, you could jump past a point on the landing hill where the landing hill "fell away." Not only could you gain more distance than jumpers without the assets, you could add a lot of feet onto the end of your jump. It was frustrating to jump on if you couldn't get over that point of the hill.

There were times when high schools tried to hold four events on a Saturday. The last event at the Holderness School was the cross country race. We finished it under automobile headlights. It was a tricky maneuver in the dark, down this long and steep hill with a 90 degree left-hand turn at the bottom. If you failed to negotiate the turn, a 20-foot drop to the highway below greeted you in the end.

Later I'll write specifically about the 80 meter Nansen Ski Jump in Berlin, New Hampshire, but I'm sure many people have forgotten the 30 meter jump(?) that was on the left side of Route 16 heading north toward the Nansen Jump. We had to take a number of turns on side streets to get back to the jump so it was not easy to find. I didn't compete on that jump. We went there for training. I believe it was a snow-less year but we had heard Berlin had a little bit of snow; I would call it ice not snow.

During my first year of college, I was hired to officiate a state meet competition hosted by Gray-New Gloucester High School. Alpine events were held at Evergreen Valley, cross country at the high school, and jumping at Hurricane Mountain, off or near Blackstrap Road in Cumberland.

When I arrived for the jumping event, I had to immediately enforce my authority as chief of hill by closing the hill; first order of business was to remove the barbed-wire fence that few jumpers could stop in time to avoid; next, we had to put snow on the landing hill where there were mostly rocks and some sand; and, after filling in a two-foot deep sag in the in-run, the jump was reopened. After that, the jumpers enjoyed the day.

I'm sure there are more jumps and places I've forgotten, however I hope this serves to bring back memories for readers and preserve the history for the future.

**Robert:**

During my years at Gould, the ski team traveled every winter to Rumford, Farmington, and Auburn for our main competition. The four schools, Rumford HS, Farmington HS, Edward Little HS, and Gould, put on winter carnivals on consecutive weekends. The four-event, team competition took place each Friday and Saturday culminating with the jumping, certainly the best event for spectators. Fans would turn out on Saturday afternoons and line the sides of the hill seeking positions from which to get the best view of the jumpers as they stretched their jumps as far down the hill as possible.

Perhaps all athletes are guilty of claiming that their glory days constituted the best era for quality of competition. I won't argue that there were some great eras for ski jumping in Maine other than the mid to late '60's but it's hard for me to believe that that era wasn't one of the best. I had to compete against the likes of Greg Cunningham, Buddy Fischer, Jim and Pat Miller, Bruce Cunningham, Gary Giberson, and George Perry from Rumford/Mexico, John and Tom Kendall from Edward Little, and

Rodney Swain, Warren Tibbets, and Mike Bates from Gould. Plus, there were the Buottes and Mansons and Zincks and Rosses.......

And I couldn't escape most of them once I was in college. Thankfully, the Millers went out West but the others attended colleges in the East, places like Dartmouth, UNH, Middlebury, and St. Lawrence. Many went on to become US Ski Team members and national champions and/or coach at prestigious schools known for their skiing prowess. Some are in ski halls of fame around the country and very few were jumping specialists; the Kendalls were threats to win any of the four events and claim the coveted skimeister crown.

Time out for a story, triggered by the name John Kendall. It takes place in 1971 or 1972 on the 50 meter jump at the Middlebury Snow Bowl, the location of the jumping for the Middlebury College Winter Carnival.

John and I were the only remaining jumpers at the top of the hill during practice jumps the day before the competition. The day had been partly sunny, therefore, we were not equipped with goggles. First understand that most preferred to jump without goggles and only used them during snowfall. Also understand that jumping without goggles was next to impossible in heavy snow.

As we stood at the top with our skis on, we could see a squall line moving in very rapidly across the valley.

John said, "Oh, no! Don't wait! Come right behind me!", as he pushed off.

I quickly shuffled to my left and jumped into the tracks behind him. When I got into my in-run position, I could see him about 30 feet ahead. When he left the takeoff, I was starting to level off and when I came out over the knoll, I could see him just landing. By the

74

time I landed, he had disappeared into the blinding snow and shortly after that, I was in white-out conditions, snowplowing for all that I was worth. I always thought it pretty cool that we trusted each other that much.

While researching, I came across two historic videos that you must see. They are truly wonderful. Just go to the Middlebury Snow Bowl website under "photos/videos" and you'll find "historic videos." One was produced in 1949 and it offers clips of many jumpers from various angles on the 40 meter jump at Chipman Hill in Middlebury along with some very good footage of skiing and winter life in and around Middlebury College. The second video spans a number of years through the 1940's and has footage from the Chipman Hill jump and the 50 meter at the Snow Bowl. It ends with Aero Skijoring on Lake Champlain. Some courageous soul is pulled across the ice/snow covered lake by a plane at 70 mph. Stop reading, right now, and go watch. You will love it.

Until 1955, we could cross the Androscoggin River from Rumford Corner to Rumford Point by ferry only. I was 7 years old when the ferry was replaced by a bridge that provided much easier access to the village of Rumford Point and the ski jump that stood on the hill behind the fire station. In order to get the lights turned on for night jumping, Dad always contacted a local jumper by the name of Jimmy Knight, who always seemed eager for a chance to jump with "Rockin' Chair" Remington and receive some pointers in the process.

**Tom:**

It was a difficult transition to Telstar after my sophomore year at Gould Academy, as far as my skiing career was concerned. I was looking forward to finishing at Gould and matching my skills up against jumpers in the highest level of school boy competition in Maine. There definitely were some quality athletes in the lower classes but the depth of competition just wasn't there and I missed the challenge of facing top jumpers on a regular basis.

If I had found a way to stay at Gould, I would have missed out on the passionate and dedicated coaching of Telstar's first ski coach, Tim LaVallee. He had a way of motivating skiers to reach their full potential and he greatly influenced my life and those of my teammates.

Many will laugh when I say that I was extremely bashful and as a result I seldom interacted with other athletes. Unfortunately, for that reason, I was perceived as being a snob and, consequently, it limited the number of fellow ski competitors who could have become lifelong friends.

It should not go unmentioned, though, that for my two years at Telstar and the years after graduation, I had the distinct honor of having as fellow ski jumping teammates outstanding individuals such as Dana Melville, Kevin Trinward, Rex Cummings, Mike and Doug Brooks, Eric Dombkowski, Mike Dunn, Doug Webster and so many more.

Maine is a long state from north to south and all too often in skiing the northern counties get forgotten. In some ways, that's odd because that region played an important role in the history of skiing in the Pine Tree State.

Lonesome Pine Ski Area in Fort Kent had a jump that I was not fortunate enough to experience. My last trip to "The County" for Class A State Interscholastic Skiing Championships (1996?) was as a ski coach. The remnants of the jump were still visible. There also was a jump in Presque Isle near Big Rock ski area. Rumor has it that

76

there was a time when the jump fell under disrepair but was revitalized before the ultimate demise of Maine interscholastic ski jumping competition. I'm sure that northern Maine had many backyard ski jumps and other jumping hills.

**Robert:**

In fact, there was a jump in Orono near the banks of the Stillwater River. It was similar to the jump behind the Andover town hall. It was a bit larger but the design was much the same including the fact that the outrun was in the flood plain of the river.

I jumped there only once. My first two years at Maine were completely dedicated to academics, cough, cough. I didn't join the team until mid to late winter of my sophomore year, the result of constant pressure applied by good friend, Dave Carter, who was inducted into the Maine Ski Hall of Fame the same night as our coach, Brud Folger. I was given the equipment I needed and I showed up at the jump the next day for an in-state competition. It all happened so fast that I'm not even sure what schools were in attendance but I believe they were Colby, Bates, and Bowdoin.

Perhaps the only reason that I remember this day is that I was recently shown a clipping from a newspaper from the day after the event. The article referred to me as "sort of a ringer" because I took second place and we won the event. I guess it was an unexpected turn of events and some of the competition were not all that happy with Coach Folger.

The Orono jump was the most easterly jump that I ever jumped on and competing on the UMaine team provided the chance to compete on many jumps throughout New England and New York. I have done some research and sadly found that many of these jumps have been destroyed. We jumped in places like the golf course jump in Hanover, NH, home of the Dartmouth College team, the Middlebury Snow Bowl, St. Lawrence University, Colby College, Williams College, Lebanon and Laconia, NH, and Bear Mountain, New York, site of the largest crowd of spectators I ever saw. Later on I will relate some stories/memories from these jumps.

The jump along the Kancamagus Highway in Conway, NH was a wonderful 30 meter hill, except for the short stopping distance of the outrun. I can't state for sure if the hill is still in use but I know that Greg Cunningham and Chuck Broomhall, products of the Chisholm Ski Club and long-time coaches at Fryeburg Academy and/or Kennett High School used and/or maintained that jump for many years. This is just another of the many examples of the influence of the Chisholm Ski Club on Nordic skiing in this country.

## Nansen Ski Jump

**Tom:**

It seems that in our family we called the 80 meter ski jump north of Berlin, New Hampshire simply The Berlin Ski Jump. It was owned and maintained by the Nansen Ski Club and played host to an annual jumping classic, one that remains affectionately forever etched in my memory.

My brother Alan, a bit more fearless than I was, made his first attempt at taking on this monster of a jump at the age of 14. Because I couldn't get the image out of my head for several weeks after his jump - him tumbling and spinning in what seemed an endless "yard sale" - I decided I would wait until I was 15. Don't misunderstand this as being some kind of remarkable feat; at that time, it was quite common.

As I've stated before, I hold fond memories of ski jumping competitions with John Phillip Sousa marches, my favorite being Stars and Stripes Forever, spewing forth from PA systems. Can you envision a human flying through the air, beautiful form, seemingly defying gravity and in the background one can hear the piccolo an octave above everything else, adding to the majesty of human flight....Sorry. Got a bit carried away.

One year required a lot of work getting the hill ready and somebody was heavily "recruited" to set tracks, followed by a couple other jumpers to help wear them into the snow.

The next jumper was US Ski Team member, Jay Martin. His flight was incredible, although I'm not so sure he thought so, especially when he realized he would out jump the landing hill. He surpassed the "K" mark on the hill by quite some distance. Upon touch down, one ski broke about half way between the boot and the tip of the ski and Martin ended in a heap, the background music coming to a halt. The silence was deafening.

Martin got to his feet, walked to the edge of the crowd, and asked where the nearest place was to purchase a new pair of skis. He made a quick trip downtown, returned with new skis, and went on to win the Class A ski jumping title that year.

In the 1940s or early 1950s, when the tower was a wooden structure, the hill was being readied for competition. A new, wet snow had fallen. The hill and tower were being readied but they needed someone to set tracks.

If you remember earlier in this book, I mentioned that in days of shellac and paraffin wax, it was always difficult to deal with all snow conditions – one of those conditions being new, wet snow.

That wasn't the only reason nobody wanted to set tracks. The old jump had a relatively short wooden ramp built perhaps 8 or 10 feet lower than the height of the end of the take-off. The ramp extended at an angle out approximately 16-20 feet. From the end of the ramp, there was a space of many feet before the start of the landing hill. (Many years later, when my brother Alan took his first jump, he barely cleared that gap.)

Finally, Dad "volunteered" to set tracks. I remember him telling the story, "I knew I was going to have a difficult time getting up enough speed to clear that gap. As soon as I shoved off, I knew for certain I would not make it, so I began dragging my hands beside me as hard as I could to slow down. When I reached the end of the take-off, I dropped onto the wooden ramp and "slued" around to a stop." He either wore holes in his gloves or he lost them part way down.

When we were perhaps 12 or 13 years of age, Sam Chapman and I decided to climb the tower – no skis, just wanted to climb the tower. We worked our way to the top - it was not my first time but his - I looked over the north side of the tower and there was the dark figure of a man lying in the snow, deep enough that he evidently could not be seen by pedestrians at ground level.

We scrambled as fast as our little feet could take us down over the tower and busted through the door of the warming hut on the same north side just behind the take-off area. Out of breath, I gasped, "I think someone has fallen off the tower and is laying in the snow out back!"

A mad scramble ensued as bodies flew out the hut door to investigate. As it turned out, it was the town drunk sleeping off the effects of too much liquid courage.

Perhaps one of the funniest events I witnessed happened when

Marshall Inman of West Paris decided to compete in the jumping at Berlin. I hadn't competed or trained hardly at all that year and I wasn't interested in sticking my neck out, but that didn't stop Marshall.

Shortly after landing on one of his rides, he ended up in a belly slide that began close to half way down the landing hill and out into the outrun for a short distance. Once he collected himself and got to his feet, he realized that the continual sliding had taken his stretch ski pants to his ankles. He quickly bent over and yanked his pants up – he was not wearing long underwear.

As soon as he got his pants yanked up nearly to his waist, he realized that they were crammed full of snow. Quickly the pants came back down and, much like someone attempting to bail water out of a rapidly sinking boat, Marshall scooped snow at a frantic pace until he thought he could pull up his pants and shake the rest out through the bottom of his cuffs. The crowd went wild.

Oh, the memories and the people who are attached to those memories on the Berlin Ski Jump over the years: Clarence "Rockin Chair' Remington, Stanley Remington, Robert Remington, Alan Remington, Peter Davis, Larry Fox, Marshall Inman, John Balfanz, Jay Martin, Roger Dion, Bernie Dion, Aurelle Legere, Norm Cummings, Art Tokle, Art Devlin, Gary Giberson, Pat Gillis, Mike Mickeriz, Ansten Samuelstuen, Jacques Charland, Robert Rasmussen, Gene Kotlarek, Larry Hodgeman, Ken Fysh, and many, many more.

And finally, it stands above the rest for it's the only jump where I exceeded 200 feet.

**Robert:**

A bit of research produced the following information on the Berlin jump. The Nansen Ski Club was founded in 1872 and is currently the oldest continuing ski club in the country. Shortly after its inception the club built a 40 meter hill and several years later remodeled it as a 45 meter.

In 1938 the club built an 80 meter hill on the site where it is located today along the Milan Road. In that inaugural year, it was the location of the US Olympic Trials. Over the years, the Nansen Ski Club maintained and improved the hill which used a 170 foot tower. They held competitions every year, including the National Championships in 1957 and 1965. Ansten Samuelstuen took the crown in 1957 and Dave Hicks in 1965. The hill closed in 1982 and has been neglected ever since but a movement is under way to refurbish it as a viewing tower/landmark.

I cannot honestly recall when I first experienced the combination of trepidation and exhilaration that came as a result of climbing that tower, strapping on the skis, riding down the in-run, and sailing over the knoll. I distinctly remember that the first several feet were very steep, so steep in fact, that keeping snow on it was nearly impossible. I never came close to eliminating the fear that I experienced standing 170 feet above the ground on a tower that moved with a gust of wind in anticipation of soaring down that steep in-run at breakneck speeds.

In 1965, my sophomore year at Gould, the Nansen Ski Club hosted the US National Championships. I was 16 years old and competed in the junior class. One of the things that jumpers were always concerned about was their place in the start order. Under most conditions, the track got faster as the day wore on so a late starting position was an advantage. I registered, picked up my numbered bib and checked the start order. I was the last junior jumper, wow! Next, I looked at the name ahead of mine. Oh, no! It was Adrian Watt from Duluth, Minnesota! He would go on to win that day and repeat as Junior National Champion the next year and as Senior National Champion in 1969. And if that wasn't enough, the jumper right behind me was John Balfanz, the reigning Senior National Champion.

The immediate future flashed before my eyes. Adrian Watt stands ready at the top of the tower. The announcer's voice erupts from loudspeakers announcing the best junior jumper in the United States. The crowd cheers in anticipation, holds its collective breath as the young phenom flies through the air, and breaks into raucous applause as he lands 265 feet down the hill. Then, I take my turn, producing applause from a dozen or so fans(thank you, family and friends) scattered among the thousands. Next, "AND NOW, THE REIGNING NATIONAL CHAMPION FROM MINNEAPOLIS, MINNESOTA, JOHN BALFANZ", and he betters Adrian Watt's jump. Sandwiched between the jumps of Misters Watt and Balfanz, I'd be lucky to get anything respectable for style points. Hell, I'd be lucky if all the judges even noticed that I was there.

But, here's what the fans and judges didn't see: We walked the side of the tower, carrying our skis, in jumping order. That made things a bit less confusing at the top. I arrived at the top platform right behind Adrian Watt and just ahead of John Balfanz. While I was bent over, buckling my boots securely into the bindings of my skis, an unusual sound caught my attention. I stood erect and twisted around to discover the dynamic duo of Watt and Balfanz retching over the rail at the back of the tower! Any amount of composure that existed within my being nearly evaporated. Mr. Balfanz must have noticed the shock on my face as he looked at me and said, "Don't worry, kid. Just a case of the nerves." Did he really think I was worried about him?

*The relic Nansen Ski Jump as can be viewed today, 2015, from the parking area across the street. Rumors have floated about that efforts are underway to restore the jump as a tourist scenic viewing venue. - Photo courtesy of Al Remington*

# Remembering "Rockin' Chair"

**Robert:**

What truly stands out in my mind from that day is the fact that my father was one of the senior jumpers. He never missed a jumping competition. By that time, I had seen him jump hundreds of times and it was as commonplace as cold and snow in winter. But now, I realize just how remarkable a time it was. You see, on that day, he jumped as a senior in the 'veterans' class for he was 40 years old!

To compensate for the fact that his aging body couldn't react as it once could, he developed a technique which allowed him the chance to continue in the sport he loved probably more than life itself. As he approached the end of the takeoff for each jump, he raised his body from a full-crouched in-run position to a semi-crouch. This provided him the chance to get into a flight position more quickly.

At the time, I thought it was strange but in later years, I realized how brilliant it was. Not only did it afford him the opportunity to continue competing, but it also allowed him the chance to be at the practice hill, jumping with and coaching his sons and all of the young aspiring jumpers that came along in the 50's, 60', and early 70's in the Western Maine area.

I was there when he took his last jump. I can't recall exactly what year it was but I do know that he was at least approaching his 50th birthday, if he hadn't, in fact, reached it. In all those years and the hundreds and possibly thousands of jumps he took, he rarely fell down. But, on that last jump, he fell and it was enough to make him hang 'em up.

**Tom:**

The landing hill at the Berlin Ski Jump was steep. After a snowfall, just one day prior to the scheduled competition, a small group of jumpers, led by Dad, strung a long "bull rope" down over the center of the landing hill. We, the volunteer packers, grabbed the rope and began packing the new snow from the top to the bottom. We held tightly to the rope leaning outward in order that our skis packed the snow as directly as possible into the hill to avoid sliding the snow toward the bottom. As I soon discovered, this was unbelievably exhausting work.

Once packed, a large, diamond shaped drag was lowered and hauled up and down the hill, by a winch, to smooth it. For its time, it was a remarkably high tech piece of equipment that saved a lot of time and manpower.

Dad was the quintessential preserver of ski jumping heritage even if he didn't know it. I think back to the many years in which he selflessly gave of himself to prepare and maintain ski jumps, and perhaps there were none so true. Even during the days when he competed regularly, he would be there to lead or follow, didn't matter. He knew the work that needed to be done before the playing began.

After he stopped competing in regular ski jumping competitions, he jumped for recreation. He loved the sport. Every Sunday afternoon, it was off to the Sunday River, Swan's Corner jump to play. However, it was work first, then play, then work again to insure the hill would be perfect for anyone who showed up after he left. It was his hill. As far as I was concerned, he owned it. It was his baby. He nursed it and cared for it. Everyone welcomed his efforts and skills. He was always visible at high school and college ski jumping competitions caring for the hill, forerunning, marking, coaching, and judging. I longed for the day the hill would receive his name. It never did.

I couldn't possibly begin to count the number of people who enjoyed and benefited from always having the Swan's Corner Jump ready for use. In addition, anyone who showed up at the jump when he was there, got free coaching. He was respected and loved. He committed himself to ski jumping and I can, without hesitation, state that had it not been for his dedication over the years, the sport of ski jumping would have ended in Maine sooner than it did.

## Stories

**Robert:**

My first story takes place at the 55 meter jump in Bear Mountain,

New York. One of my teammates, while on the team at Maine, was a young man by the name of Mike Fendler. Mike was a relative of Don Fendler, the boy *"Lost On A Mountain In Maine"*. Mike joined the team with little experience and coaching but with plenty of talent and enthusiasm. His early learning curve was steep and he advanced rapidly.

Bear Mountain is a reasonable drive north of New York City and the annual Sunday afternoon jumping tournament brought out thousands of city folk to witness the 'crazies' fly through the air. I never jumped in front of a crowd that large.

It was a beautiful, sunny day with no wind and everything was perfect conditions for jumping and spectating. The vast majority of the crowd gathered behind a roped-off barrier that surrounded the outrun. After completing our jumps and coming to a stop at the end of the outrun we could literally be "up close and personal" with the audience.

After finishing my first jump, I stood, surrounded by the throng, and waited for Mike to complete his first competition round. As I watched, I saw him "hit the take-off" and sail well down the hill – without a doubt the best jump of his life. I was excited for him and couldn't wait to "high-five" him and share his celebration. I was soon to find out that the excitement of sharing the celebration of success could quickly turn to embarrassment as Mike came to a stop, tilted his head back, and while looking to the heavens, shouted over the noise of the crowd, "THAT WAS BETTER THAN SEX!"

**Tom:**

When Dad was deeply involved in the Pineland Ski Club, there were monthly meetings, quite often held in the old Town Hall on Elm St., across from the Congregational Church. The approximate time frame on this story was around 1960-1965.

Sometimes when Dad was heading for a meeting in Andover, we would hound him until he agreed to let us go. We would load our jumping skis into the back of the truck, pile into the cab – no need for seat belts - and head to Andover.

The Elm Street jump stood behind the town hall. We turned the lights on and jumped while he was in his meeting. Sometimes when we were there, we might run into some other locals - Bruce Simmons, Joel Hodgdon, Kerry Meisner, Paula and Penny Poor, Brandon Falkenham, Alston Roberts, Roger Mills, Kenny Jodrey, Rodney Swain – stopping by for a few rides.

One night on our way into town, we stopped at my cousin Bruce Simmons' house at the lower end of Main Street. He, too, was eager to go with us to the Town Hall and have some fun ski jumping under the lights.

On the side of the building facing the jump was a fairly large wooden box. It contained the light switch for the jump. We switched on the lights and walked over to the hill and started taking rides.

When cousin, Bruce, left the top of the tower on one of his turns and was about half way down, the lights went out. You can imagine our surprise and fright, suddenly going from bright lights to full darkness. Bruce wasn't as surprised as he was mad. I can still hear him carrying on about the event and justifiably so.

When the lights didn't come back on, we felt our way over to the side of the building and discovered the switch had been turned to the off position. "Who could have done such a thing?"

Bruce was still fuming as he walked out front of the Hall where he met up with one Gabby Porter, one of the local "characters."

Bruce blurted, "Did you turn off the lights on the jump a few minutes ago?"

Now, Gabby was a tobacco chewer and didn't necessarily dress like the town mayor. His clothes were somewhat disheveled, sporting a scraggly, crusty and tobacco-stained beard – he may or may not have had any teeth. Gabby snapped to attention, got into Bruce's space, and announced, "I shut out the lights..." to which there was a pause while he turned his head slightly to his left, spit a wad of nasty, black, tobacco juice and finished, "Any questions?"

We stood in anticipation of Bruce's response. Would he boil over and explode? Would he become violent? Would profanity ring throughout the village? No, he laughed.....and laughed....and we joined him!

We decided that we had better call it a night, loaded our skis into Dad's truck, and walked down the street to Bruce's house where we would be picked up later.

Upon entering his house Bruce began his story and pantomime, repeating verbatim mimicking all Gabby's gestures, complete with the spitting on his mother's floor. Oops!

**Robert:**

It was the winter of 1972 and we were jumping on the 55 meter hill at Black Mountain, commonly known as the Aurele Legere jump. In a previous story, I wrote about the fact that the University of Vermont had two Norwegians on their jumping team. Now, keep in mind that ski jumping is a Nordic sport, like cross country skiing, named most likely because its origins are Norwegian.

This fact would allow a Norwegian to believe that he inherited the sense of what is good, just, and maybe even holy in the sport of ski jumping, and Americans, being neophytes(for decades or longer?), did not possess the inherited knowledge of the beautifully artistic sport borne of the Norwegian culture.

I can just imagine a situation that would be the reversal of that day at the top of the tower of the Legere hill: I'm in a dugout of a baseball field in Lillehammer, Norway playing baseball for a Norwegian baseball team. At age 22, my view of the playing field would most likely involve some amount of condescension and I might say something that would reflect that attitude.

Okay, let's flash back to Rumford. It's a cloudy day with no wind. The tower is a wooden structure. There's enough wood in it to frame up several houses. It must have taken countless hours of labor to build. It was not pretty. As a matter of fact, it was ugly. It probably had no help from an architect, for an architect would certainly have made it a thing of beauty at a cost that the Chisholm Ski Club could never afford.

But, I do believe that beauty *is* in the eye of the beholder for I – and I'm sure all of my American comrades – felt it was a Taj Mahal of ski jumps for it provided a wonderful ride. From the surface of the snow through the air above, it was a most pleasurable experience riding down the in-run, off the takeoff, and over the knoll into the air above the landing hill. We couldn't have cared less what the structure looked like.

I was putting on my skis in preparation for my first practice ride of the day when I heard the heavy, Nordic accent of a voice beside me, "Dis es crazy."

I was an extremely shy person at that time and completely intimidated by the Norwegians, so I simply said, "What?"

He answered, "Sheeing on dis," as he nodded in the direction of the tower.

Mine was a wordless response. I scowled, looked at the tower, looked back at him, and shrugged.

To which he added, "In my country, dis would be condemned."

"*I* like it," was all I could come up with as I pushed off and bounced into my in-run position.

**Tom:**

Speaking of pushing off and bouncing into an in-run position, I am reminded of a ski jumper who had a habit of pushing off and just before "bouncing into an in-run position," clapped his gloved hands together – I suppose some form of "getting psyched up."

On day right after completing his "clap", the jumper realized that the hook and ring on the two gloves had become joined. The remainder of the ride was comical to say the least.

When strange events occur during ski jumping competition, it can be comical for spectators but certainly not for the jumper. One Saturday, during a jumping meet at the Swan's Corner Jump, the snow was rock hard. The jump was well-covered with snow but we might have had some rain which had frozen rock solid; boiler plate it is called.

Before any jumping was to take place, iron rakes were manned and attempts were made to scratch the surface of the landing hill in hopes that it would roughen it up enough to help provide a bit of ski stability upon touch down.

Later on a jumper, upon the hard impact with skis onto the landing hill, broke his ski. As would be discovered in a few minutes, the skier's right ski had cracked across the width of it approximately a foot and a half back from the tip.

But, the jumper didn't notice and during his second jump, as he headed down the in-run, the broken ski was digging into the track and shooting a rooster tail of ice and snow up into the skier's face. A long splinter of wood from the ski, somehow, was left behind, sticking up out of the snow right in the ski track.

The jumper finished his jump and returned to the top of the hill for his last jump... with the same skis. Somebody handed him a roll of athletic tape and he wrapped a couple of times around the ski and headed for the top. Another jumper ask, "Are you going to jump again with those skis?" The jumper replied, "Yeah, I think so. I hope the tape will help keep the snow out of my face." Ski jumpers are a breed aren't they? Perhaps a bit dystopic?

Another "comical" incident happened on the same ski jump. The jumper was Gary Inman from Oxford Hills High School. Gary grew up in West Paris and spent many hours jumping on homemade jumps in the neighborhood. I wrote about some of those earlier on. Gary seemed to have little fear of ski jumping. After all, if there were not trees and other obstacles to avoid while jumping, how scary could it be?

Some might not understand this mindset, but we grew up this way and when it came time to push off the top and get into the in-run tracks, we always looked for ways to be aggressive. Sometimes there would be hand rails to grab hold of. The jumper would kick and pull to get up to speed as quickly as possible. Speed could mean the difference of one foot in distance, which might mean another position in the final results.

The Swan's Corner Jump didn't have hand rails to grab but it did have a kick board at the back of the tower structure. A jumper that wished to use the kick board, would place one ski back to rest upon the board and kick off with that ski to gain speed.

A common binding or foot harness for jumping skis back in the 1960s was called a "bear trap" binding. An actual bear trap might have been better. The toe of the boot went into a metal contraption that could be adjusted to fit the size and shape of the toe of the boot. It had two sides of metal. To keep the toe of the boot in the "trap" it had either a leather strap over the top of the boot – sometimes a piece of string, baling twine, inner tube or jar rubber - or the evolution of the equipment began providing metal "clips" on both sides of the side pieces that fit over the top of the outer part of the sole of the boot. This prevented the boot from coming up and out of the trap – provided, of course, that the sole of the boot remained attached to the upper boot and tied securely to the foot. Don't laugh.

There was also a metal cable with a "U-shaped" spring at the back that was placed on the heel of the jumping boot. A lever in front of the toe trap was used to clamp the boot into the binding by cinching the cable tight. This cable was adjustable and each jumper would make adjustments that fit his style of ski jumping. This was important to allow the ski to follow the desired flight pattern through the air.

When Gary aggressively shoved off at the top, the ski, boot and leg he placed against the kick board to kick with, created enough force that his foot came out of the binding. Off he went...on one ski and not really knowing what he ought to do. He decided to try to ride it out. He remained mostly in a standing position and rode on his one ski to the end of the take-off. He went a short distance through the air, landed, mostly on the foot with the ski on it, went a short distance, and fell, unharmed.

All of this is quite remarkable, but as time went by I thought about this and decided that, knowing Gary and the Inman family in general, it surely would not surprise me to learn that when not in competition, he tried this trick before.

**Tom:**

This has been a joy for me. I tried, with the best of my abilities and knowledge, to remember as much information about ski jumping in Western Maine, even risking a journey or two beyond the comforts of home, in hopes that my work will do to you what it did for me – trigger memories and wonderful thoughts.

It is my heart-felt intent that this effort on my part and that of my brother, and anyone else who played a role in providing some information, helps to establish another small archive of information to share with those interested in history and, in particular, the sport of ski jumping. Thank you.

# Ski Jumping History References

1. Bethel Journals – Swan's Corner Jump - http://www.thebetheljournals.info/SwansCornerJump.htm

2. Andover Journals – Pictures and Information - http://andoverjournal.net/oldwinterpics.html

3. Middlebury Snow Bowl – Historic Videos - http://www.middleburysnowbowl.com/historic-videos/

4. Ski Jumping in the Eastern U.S.A. - http://www.skijumpeast.com/skiclubs.htm - http://www.skijumpeast.com/genintro.htm

5. Book: Words for a Mountain – Richard Kent – History of Skiing Rumford, Maine - http://www.amazon.com/Words-Mountain-Richard-Kent/dp/0986019143/ref=sr_1_1? s=books&ie=UTF8&qid=1426521644&sr=1-1&keywords=words+for+a+mountain

6. Ski Jumping Hill Archive – List of Jumps in the U.S.A. - http://www.skisprungschanzen.com/EN/Ski+Jumps/USA-United+States/

Made in the USA
Middletown, DE
22 July 2015